THE
OCEANS
A CELEBRATION

WAVES BREAKING

(Kim Westerskov)

OVERLEAF: A SCHOOL OF FUSILIERS OVER A CHALICE CORAL

(David Hall)

THE
OCEANS

A CELEBRATION

A CORAL GROUPER
(Jeffrey L. Rotman)

COMPILED BY THE LIVING EARTH FOUNDATION

Editor: LISA SILCOCK

Commissioning Editor: DAMIEN LEWIS   Consultant Editor: ROBERT BISSET

Introduction by DAVID BELLAMY

CRESCENT BOOKS

NEW YORK · AVENEL, NEW JERSEY

FIRST PUBLISHED IN UK 1993

THIS 1993 EDITION PUBLISHED BY
CRESCENT BOOKS, DISTRIBUTED BY
OUTLET BOOK COMPANY, INC.,
A RANDOM HOUSE COMPANY
40 ENGELHARD AVENUE
AVENEL, NEW JERSEY 07001

RANDOM HOUSE
NEW YORK   TORONTO   LONDON   SYDNEY   AUCKLAND

DESIGNER: DAVID FORDHAM
CO-ORDINATING EDITOR: SUE PHILLPOTT

ISBN 0–517–10326–5

PRINTED IN ITALY BY OFFICINE GRAFICHE DE AGOSTINI, NOVARA

CONTENTS

INTRODUCTION 7
PROFESSOR DAVID BELLAMY

CHAPTER 1
BEYOND THE MIRROR SURFACE: THE OCEAN ECOSYSTEM 9
DR JULIAN CALDECOTT

CHAPTER 2
THE BEAUTIFUL AND THE BIZARRE: AN UNPARALLELED DIVERSITY 35
DR TUNDI AGARDY

CHAPTER 3
THE PLANKTON POWERHOUSE: ENERGY CAPTURE IN THE SEA 57
DR IAN JOINT

CHAPTER 4
PILOTS OF THE OPEN OCEAN: THE GREAT MARINE MIGRATIONS 77
MARK SIMMONDS

CHAPTER 5
EAT OR BE EATEN: GAMBLING FOR SURVIVAL 93
DR MARTIN ANGEL

CHAPTER 6
DANCING IN THE DARK: SIGNALLING IN A SUNLESS WORLD 111
DR PETER HERRING

CHAPTER 7
FROM ATMOSPHERE TO ABYSS: THE ENDLESS CYCLE OF ELEMENTS 129
DR ANDREW WATSON

CHAPTER 8
MOVING MOUNTAINS: THE DYNAMIC OCEAN FLOOR 155
SIR ANTHONY LAUGHTON

CHAPTER 9
LIFE ON THE EDGE: A MOSAIC OF ECOSYSTEMS 171
DR NICHOLAS POLUNIN

CHAPTER 10
THE HUMAN OCEANS: PROTECTORS AND PLUNDERERS 197
PROFESSOR ALASTAIR COUPER

CONCLUSION 219
ROGER HAMMOND

THE LIVING EARTH FOUNDATION 220

LIST OF CONTRIBUTORS 221

ACKNOWLEDGEMENTS 222

INDEX 225

INTRODUCTION

Professor David Bellamy

Salt water covers seventy per cent of planet earth to an average depth of four thousand metres (13,000 ft). A proportion of this vast volume of liquid escapes as pure vapour into the atmosphere, and some is blown over the land as clouds. Every day, these clouds moisten our otherwise dry islands and continents and replenish our rivers with eighty cubic kilometres (19 cubic miles) of fresh water, shed as rain, sleet or snow. All life depends utterly on water, and this process, which begins and ends in the sea, supplies it to every organism on land: that is, to every plant, to every animal, and to a human population now approaching six billion.

Our intimate relationship with the sea goes back three and a half billion years, when life as we know it began to develop in the oceans. Today, the sea is home to about half of all the species of plants and animals, discounting the insects, that inhabit our planet. From the smallest to the largest, each has a vital part to play in maintaining the balance of life on earth.

Swarms of microscopic algae known as coccolithophores, for example, manufacture protective crystal shells using carbon dioxide. Their skeletons, along with the bodies of other creatures, fall in a constant rain into the abyssal depths. Tiny corals also use carbon dioxide to build their great limestone reefs. Thus these minute creatures lock up great quantities of the most abundant greenhouse gas in the depths of the sea, out of harm's way – and produce oxygen into the bargain.

At the opposite end of the scale, we are at last learning that the great whales and their kin have more to offer us alive than dead. For the present, this is one of conservation's success stories, and most people now abhor the idea of killing these sentient, highly intelligent creatures, whose behaviour offers many parallels with our own: whales 'talk' to each other, make love, live in family groups, teach their children and even sing complex songs. Yet a few 'cultured' and very rich nations want to resume hunting, claiming that whales can be harvested on a scientifically sustainable basis. A harpoon often takes many hours to kill even a small minke whale, while its family looks on in distress.

It is clear that despite hard campaigning by world experts and hundreds of thousands of other intelligent people, the message still has not got through to many of those most responsible for the oceans. As I write this, thousands of birds, otters, seals, fish and other creatures are endangered by the oil leaking from a tanker aground on the Shetland coast. It is, say the authorities, another accident that should not have happened: but what are they doing about preventing the next one, and about marine conservation as a whole?

Time is running out for the oceans. Please read this book, because the extraordinary life that it celebrates is exactly what is at stake. Then join the campaigners and help us to fight for the oceans' survival: for their own sake, for yourselves and for your children's future.

A GREY ANGEL FISH, GRAND BAHAMA
(Richard Herrmann)

7

CHAPTER ONE

BEYOND THE MIRROR SURFACE: THE OCEAN ECOSYSTEM
Dr Julian Caldecott

It's easy to think of the world's surface in the old way: as a pattern of land, with emptiness in between. Realization can come suddenly, though. Maybe while watching waves explode against a rugged coastline, or when snorkelling or scuba diving; perhaps in the first few seconds after the cold plunge from a dinghy, when you roll over and look down at the other two thirds of Creation. After that, it's all different.

IMAGINE: YOU ARE DEEP IN TRANSPARENT WATER, BESIDE a rocky wall off, say, the coast of Sulawesi, Indonesia. The wall is encrusted with corals, sponges, tentacled anemones, sea-squirts and algae; the seabed is invisibly far below, the mirror surface high above. A spectacular array of swimming creatures glide and dart around you. There is a giant spotted eagle-ray; some blue surgeonfish, and clown triggerfish; a dense pack of several hundred blackfin barracuda; banded sea-snakes; green turtles; gigantic Napoleon wrasse; torrents of small, bright lunar fusiliers; masses of silver jacks and trevallies; even white-tipped reef sharks.

At night, by flashlight, you see different creatures: mantis shrimps, delicately branching gorgonians, feather-stars, spiny lobsters, and parrotfish sleeping in bags of mucus within little caves. There are brittle-stars creeping, sea-stars feeding, and urchins waving their pencil-thick spines. Before, this rock wall was just a darker line in the sea, perhaps glanced at from an aeroplane window. Now, you hesitate to order seafish from a

---

1 A GARIBALDI, CATALINA ISLAND, CALIFORNIA
(Richard Herrmann)
A SHALLOW-WATER DAMSELFISH WHICH USUALLY INHABITS KELP FORESTS, THE GARIBALDI IS EXTREMELY TERRITORIAL. THE MALE GUARDS THE EGGS, MAKING DEEP GUTTURAL SOUNDS WHEN AGITATED, AND WILL CHARGE POTENTIAL PREDATORS, NO MATTER WHAT THEIR SIZE. FORMERLY THREATENED BY ENTHUSIASTIC COLLECTING FOR AQUARIUMS, THE GARIBALDI IS NOW THE STATE MARINE FISH OF CALIFORNIA, AND IS OFFICIALLY PROTECTED.

restaurant menu; you wonder about how the sea works, and with it, the world.

The ocean waters cover two thirds of our planet's surface, circling the world in unbroken continuity. They are the ballast and buffer of earth's ecology, the birthplace of its plants and animals, and the major store of living resources and chemicals necessary for life. The seas stabilize the atmosphere, and are the source of the weather which affects us on land. They remain, however, largely unknown: much research is still needed to identify their inhabitants and to understand their ecology. Our lack of knowledge is a product not only of the sea's inaccessibility, but also of its fundamental *difference*. For to penetrate the glittering surface of the sea is to enter an alien realm, where entirely new rules of biological diversity and energy flow apply.

From our terrestrial viewpoint, we tend to think of biological diversity in terms of trees and ferns, birds and mammals. But unless you venture beneath the sea you will never encounter almost half of the fundamental kinds of living creature that exist on our planet. Zoology distinguishes thirty-three different animal phyla in the world, each phylum representing a basic life-form design. The oceans are host to thirty-two of these phyla, fifteen of which are *exclusively* marine.

Many oceanic life forms look truly extraordinary to our eyes, accustomed only to creatures adapted to terrestrial living. For example, the floating pink siphonophore looks like a translucent eyeball with a blue iris. It pulsates up and down as it drifts, controlling its buoyancy by secreting carbon monoxide into its float. Behind it trail some 10 metres (over 30 ft) of fine, contractile, stinging tentacles: a deadly trap for prey.

Shapes mislead: the pale, graceful little 'plants' on the coral wall are actually animals – sea-fan hydroids. The multi-tentacled 'worm' foraging over the coral is as much a mollusc as is the garden slug; it has stolen the stinging cells of its prey and incorporated them into its tentacles for its own defence. The pieces of fine white cloth clinging to the sharp edge of the reef are not rags, but animals – membranous ribbon bryozoans.

The apparently bizarre appearance of such life forms is, though, as logical an evolutionary solution to conditions in the sea as the legs of animals are to life on land. For instance, because sea-water supports living tissue, floating or weak-swimming marine organisms do not need the heavy skeletons required to support land plants and animals. Many sea creatures are delicate and jelly-like; jellyfish are familiar examples. Furthermore, the physical structure and lifestyle of every marine organism reflects its place in the ocean. The sea provides a much more three-dimensional environment than the land, with a far greater volume of space available for use by living organisms. This space is extremely varied in the conditions it provides for its inhabitants: light, temperature, salinity, nutrient concentration and pressure all differ greatly with place and time.

In shallow waters, for example, light is plentiful. Here the variety of colour and form is astonishing. Consider the rippling purple and orange blotches of the leopard flatworm; the goofy-mouthed, colour-changing scribbled filefish; or the intricate blue-black-gold *cloisonné* work of the 'male' (actually sex-reversed) spotted boxfish. In these high-visibility waters, such gaudiness is no evolutionary accident. Markings may serve as camouflage; but bright, distinctive patterns are more often visual signals, indicating a poisonous nature to would-be predators, or advertising the species identity, sexual status or social rank of individuals.

Above 100 metres (330 ft) or so, there is enough light to support photosynthesis – the process by which plants convert sunlight and atmospheric gases into organic materials for growth. Here, microscopic free-floating plants called phytoplankton proliferate. These form the base of marine food chains, directly or indirectly supporting every one of the sea's creatures. The energy harnessed by plant plankton is passed on to the many tiny animals which prey on them – the so-called zooplankton, including minute shrimps, sticky-armed ctenophorans, and innumerable marine larvae. Zooplankton are, in turn, the staple diet of filter-feeding creatures – from corals, sponges and tiny fish fry to the enormous whale-shark and the great baleen whales themselves.

Above filter-feeders in the food chain comes an amazing array of secondary consumers. These include multi-species aggregations of brilliantly coloured parrotfish, which can crush corals like biscuits in their fused, beak-like teeth, and the omnivorous Picasso triggerfish – known to Hawaiians as *humuhumu-nukunuku-a-pua'a*: 'the fish which grunts like a pig'. More specialized is the crown-of-thorns starfish, which everts its stomach through its mouth to envelop and digest coral polyps.

Continue up the predator hierarchy, to fish which pounce from the sky at dusk and dawn – like the crocodile needlefish, which has been known to impale fishermen in their boats. Others ambush from cover, or stalk the bottom at night. The sequence ends with top predators which have no need of such subtleties: the killer whale, the great barracuda, and the aptly named requiem sharks. Still other creatures target the dead or the dying, contributing to the dramatic rate with which life in the ocean is recycled. Unconsumed dead plankton and animal carcasses become drifting and sedimenting resources for foragers like heart-urchins, sea cucumbers, shrimps and crabs. The remaining debris drifts downwards five km (3 miles) or more, where it becomes food for a vast number of deep-living species.

Sediment from the remains of ocean life gradually accumulates as a shroud over the seabed, mixing with sand, eventually to settle and harden into layers of rock. Older seabeds, reflecting many millions of years of prehuman history, can be seen when reconstructed from seismic surveys. These provide clues to the dynamic, impermanent nature of the oceans and of the earth itself. Here is the crest of a fossilized coral reef or islet, once overwhelmed by rising sea levels and gradually covered by new layers of rock; there, a gentle dome over the remains of prehistoric vegetation long since buried.

Constantly shifting and undulating, the seabed has altered dramatically over hundreds of millions of years. Continents have moved and whole sections have been swallowed. Huge volcanic mountain ranges, their tips sometimes emerging as islands above the sea, have appeared; elsewhere, the ancient ocean crust has been squeezed back down into the earth's fiery interior. Sea levels rise and fall: just 20,000 years ago, they were 130 metres (430 ft) lower than today, and dry land linked much of the Indonesian archipelago to Asia and Australia.

Dramatic though they are, these are natural changes which have taken place over millions of years, and ecosystems have tended to adapt themselves accordingly. However, there are some changes, brought about by our own species, that they cannot accommodate. Human societies throughout history have differed widely in their willingness to maintain natural systems by using them sustainably, and in their ability to do harm. On the one hand, there are healthy mangroves which have undergone a thousand years' use by fisherfolk and collectors of such products as thatching materials, charcoal, seaweed, palm sugar, honey, fish and shellfish. On the other, there are crippled wildernesses of acidic mud left from a dozen years' clearfelling of mangroves for rayon pulp and disposable chop-sticks. Coastal settlements have often been the springboards of civilization, trade, colonization and conquest. Alien life forms and alien values have been introduced, wreaking ecological witchcraft on the life and very substance of the world's ocean systems.

The ecology, geology, biogeography and sociology of the oceans constitute a vital part of the human and natural history of our planet. The influence of the oceans has been decisive in the past, and will be equally so in the future. It is to the many roles of the oceans that this book is dedicated, as a celebration – with affection, astonishment, respect and hope.

---

2 ORANGE SEA-PERCH OVER A CORAL REEF, RED SEA

(Linda Pitkin)

THESE FISH, SOMETIMES CALLED 'BASSLETS', ARE COMMON IN THE SHALLOW
WATERS ABOVE THE RED SEA REEFS (THIS ONE IS OFF THE COAST OF EGYPT).
SMALL NUMBERS OF MAGENTA-COLOURED MALES PRESIDE OVER LARGE HAREMS
OF ORANGE FEMALES.

3

3   A BARRACUDA, GRAND CAYMAN, WEST INDIES

(J. Michael Kelly)

BARRACUDA CAN REACH 30 KG (66 LB) OR MORE IN WEIGHT AND ARE FEROCIOUS
PREDATORS, EQUIPPED WITH LARGE JAWS AND RAZOR-SHARP TEETH. THEY HUNT
ALONE OR IN SMALL SCHOOLS, CRUISING AROUND THE REEF EDGE IN SEARCH OF
STRAY FISH, WHICH THEY PURSUE RELENTLESSLY. SOMETIMES THEY WILL ALSO
EAT CARRION. SOME TWENTY SPECIES ARE FOUND WORLDWIDE, MAINLY IN
TROPICAL SEAS. IN SOME WATERS THEY HAVE BEEN KNOWN TO ATTACK
SWIMMERS AND DIVERS, BUT THIS IS PROBABLY A CASE OF MISTAKEN IDENTITY:
THE FLASH OF A WATCH MAY RESEMBLE A DARTING FISH. BARRACUDAS
THEMSELVES ARE OFTEN HUNTED BY HUMANS FOR THEIR MEAT.

4

4   A TARPON AMONGST A SCHOOL OF SILVERSIDES

(J. Michael Kelly)

THOUGH THEY PREFER SHALLOWS AND MANGROVE FLATS, TARPON ARE OFTEN FOUND DRIFTING THROUGH THE CANYONS AND CAVES OF THE CARIBBEAN REEFS AT DEPTHS OF 12-18 METRES (40-60 FT). THEY CAN GROW TO A LENGTH OF 2 METRES (6.5 FT). GOLDFISH-SIZED SILVERSIDES DRIFT THROUGH THE SAME CAVES AND CANYONS IN DENSE SCHOOLS. WHEN NIGHT FALLS, BOTH SPECIES ABANDON THEIR DEEPER DAYTIME HABITATS TO FEED CLOSER TO THE SURFACE, PLUNGING BACK DOWN AGAIN AS DAY BREAKS.

5

5   A BLUE COD SWALLOWING A WRASSE

(Darryl Torckler/Tony Stone Worldwide)

PREDATORY FISH SUCH AS THE BLUE COD PATROL THE DEEPER WATERS AROUND CORAL REEFS, SEIZING INCAUTIOUS PREY LIKE THIS WRASSE.

7

6   A SEA-FAN, CARIBBEAN

(Linda Pitkin)

SEA-FANS ARE COLONIES OF CORALS KNOWN AS GORGONIANS, OR HORNY
CORALS; THEY HAVE A MUCH MORE FLEXIBLE CASING THAN THE REEF-FORMING
STONY VARIETY. PURPLE SEA-FANS ARE ABUNDANT THROUGHOUT THE
CARIBBEAN. THEY TYPICALLY LIVE DEEPER DOWN THE FACE OF THE REEF,
WHERE THE WATER IS COOLER AND THE SUNLIGHT THINNER. GROWING AT RIGHT
ANGLES TO THE PREVAILING CURRENT, FANS STRAIN MICROSCOPIC PARTICLES OF
FOOD FROM THE WATER. THE TENTACLES OF THE POLYPS – THE MULTITUDES OF
TINY UNITS THAT MAKE UP THE FAN – MAKE IT VIRTUALLY IMPOSSIBLE FOR ANY
SMALL DRIFTING ORGANISM TO PASS SAFELY BY.

7   A GORGONIAN, CUBA

(Linda Pitkin)

HORNY CORALS ARE FOUND GROWING ALL OVER REEFS OF STONY CORAL. THEY
MAY BE FAN-SHAPED (6), WHIP-LIKE, BUSHY OR PLUME-LIKE, AS HERE. MORE
FLEXIBLE GORGONIANS SUCH AS THIS ONE CAN WITHSTAND QUITE STRONG
CURRENTS THAT WOULD DESTROY THE MORE BRITTLE, DELICATE SEA-FAN.

8

8   A LONG-NOSE HAWKFISH IN GORGONIAN CORAL, INDO-PACIFIC

(Norbert Wu)

WITH THEIR REMARKABLE PATTERNING, THESE HAWKFISH ARE ADMIRABLY
DISGUISED WITHIN THE RED GORGONIANS' BRANCHES, WHERE THEY ARE
COMMONLY SEEN – THOUGH THEY ARE ALSO FOUND ON BLACK CORAL. THEIR
CAMOUFLAGE NOT ONLY PROTECTS THEM FROM PREDATORS, BUT ALSO ENABLES
THEM TO AMBUSH THEIR PREY – USUALLY SMALL CRUSTACEANS.

9   A PARROTFISH, BORNEO

(Norbert Wu)

THERE ARE MANY SPECIES OF THESE BRILLIANT FISH. THEY LIVE AROUND CORAL
REEFS, AND THE LARGEST GROW TO ONE METRE (OVER 3 FT) OR MORE. MOST ARE
GRAZERS, SCRAPING CORAL FROM THE REEFS AND CRUNCHING IT IN THEIR
SHARP MOUTHPARTS IN ORDER TO EXTRACT THE POLYPS WITHIN IT. THE
PULVERIZED CORAL THAT THEY EXCRETE CONTRIBUTES TO THE SILT AROUND
REEFS. SOME PARROTFISH SLEEP DRAPED IN A MUCUS COVERING, WHICH
PROBABLY HELPS THEM TO AVOID BEING DETECTED BY PREDATORS. LIKE ALL
THE WRASSES, SOME FEMALE PARROTFISH CHANGE SEX, BECOMING BRIGHTLY
PATTERNED MALES.

9

10 A SEA HORSE, SEA OF CORTEZ
(Mark Conlin/Planet Earth)
SEA HORSES INHABIT SHALLOW
COASTAL WATERS AROUND THE
REEFS OF TROPICAL AND WARM
TEMPERATE SEAS. THEY HAVE
PREHENSILE TAILS, WITH WHICH
THEY ANCHOR THEMSELVES TO
SEAWEEDS, CORAL AND SPONGES.
THEIR EYES MOVE INDEPENDENTLY
LIKE THOSE OF CHAMELEONS ON
LAND, PERMITTING THEM TO SCAN
TWO DIRECTIONS AT ONCE, FOR
FOOD AND FOR PREDATORS. SEA
HORSES HAVE NO TEETH, BUT WITH
THEIR ELONGATED SNOUTS THEY
SUCK IN THE SHRIMPS AND
COPEPODS ON WHICH THEY FEED.

10

**11   A SLENDER FILEFISH IN
GORGONIAN CORAL, BELIZE**
(Michael J. Kelly)
THE SLENDER FILEFISH IS FOUND
MAINLY IN THE CARIBBEAN. TWO
TO 6 CM (1-2 IN) LONG, IT USUALLY
LIVES CAMOUFLAGED IN
GORGONIANS (AS HERE),
POSITIONED VERTICALLY; BUT IT
MAY SOMETIMES BE SEEN ON
SEAGRASS BEDS, IN ROCKY- OR
SANDY-BOTTOMED WATERS. SOME
SPECIES OF FILEFISH CAN VARY
THEIR COLOUR TO MATCH THEIR
SURROUNDINGS. THEIR DIET IS
VERY VARIED, AND INCLUDES
SPONGES, HYDROIDS AND
STINGING CORAL.

11

12

12   A RED IRISH LORD, VANCOUVER ISLAND

(Linda Pitkin)

DESPITE ITS BRIGHT COLOURING, THIS FISH IS WELL DISGUISED IN ITS ROCKY
SEA-FLOOR HABITAT IN THE TEMPERATE WATERS OF NORTH AMERICA'S PACIFIC
COAST. THERE IT LIES, WAITING TO AMBUSH CRUSTACEANS, MOLLUSCS AND
SMALL FISH THAT STRAY TOO NEAR. SINCE IT INHABITS COASTAL WATERS, IT IS
SUSCEPTIBLE TO THE DUMPING OF WASTES AND TO RUN-OFF FROM THE LAND.

13

13   A STARRY PUFFERFISH, SOLOMON ISLANDS

(B. Jones & M. Shimlock)

ALSO KNOWN AS THE WHITE-SPOTTED PUFFER OR STARS-AND-STRIPES PUFFER,
THIS SOLITARY FISH MAY GROW UP TO 50 CM (20 IN). IT IS A POOR SWIMMER, AND
USUALLY RESIDES NEAR THE SEA FLOOR IN SHALLOWISH WATERS. LIKE ALL
PUFFERS, IT INFLATES ITSELF, WHEN ALARMED, BY DRAWING WATER INTO A
POUCH NEAR ITS STOMACH. IT IS FAIRLY COMMON IN THE INDO-PACIFIC, AS FAR
NORTH AS JAPAN.

14 *ACROPORA* CORAL, SOLOMON ISLANDS

(Norbert Wu)

CORALS OF THE GENUS *ACROPORA* ADOPT MORE GROWTH FORMS THAN ANY OTHER, WITH THE SAME SPECIES BEING FOUND IN STAGHORN, PLATE, TABULAR AND BRANCHING SHAPES. VIGOROUS GROWERS, THEY ARE THE DOMINANT COLONIZING CORALS ON MOST REEFS, AND ARE AMONG THE FIRST TO OCCUPY NEW HABITATS SUCH AS UNDERSEA LAVA FLOWS. THEY CAN LIVE ONLY IN SHALLOW WATER, HOWEVER, WHERE THE SUNLIGHT IS STRONG ENOUGH FOR THE SYMBIOTIC ALGAE (ZOOXANTHELLAE) WHICH INHABIT CORAL POLYPS TO PHOTOSYNTHESIZE, THUS PROVIDING FOOD FOR THE CORAL ITSELF. TO PREVENT DEHYDRATION WHEN EXPOSED DURING LOW TIDES, THE CORAL SECRETES A PROTECTIVE MUCUS.

15

15 A GIANT GREEN ANEMONE, SAN MIGUEL ISLAND, CALIFORNIA

(Richard Herrmann)

THE CARNIVOROUS ANEMONE'S TENTACLES ARE ARMED WITH STINGING CELLS
THAT ARE LETHAL TO SMALL CREATURES. THE TENTACLES PUSH THE DEAD PREY
INTO THE CENTRAL MOUTH. THE GIANT GREEN IS CONSIDERED THE CLASSIC
PACIFIC ANEMONE. UNLIKE MOST, WHICH LIVE BELOW THE TIDAL ZONE AND ARE
CONTINUALLY UNDER WATER, THESE CAN BE FOUND EXPOSED IN TIDAL POOLS
ALONG THE CALIFORNIAN COAST. AT NIGHT THEY FOLD THEIR TENTACLES INSIDE
THEIR BODIES FOR PROTECTION.

16

16 A TUBE CORAL POLYP, PHILIPPINES

(David Hall)

THOUGH TECHNICALLY ONE OF THE HARD CORALS, TUBE CORALS DO NOT FORM THE CLOSE COLONIES THAT BUILD REEFS, BUT GROW A FEW CENTIMETRES APART FROM EACH OTHER. AT NIGHT, THE POLYPS EMERGE FROM THEIR HARD TUBES AND EXTEND THEIR STINGING TENTACLES TO FEED ON THE MINUTE ORGANISMS DRIFTING BY. AT FULL STRETCH, EACH POLYP MAY BE 5 CM (2 IN) LONG.

17

17 AN ORANGE BALL CORALLIMORPH, GRAND CAYMAN

(J. Michael Kelly)

DESPITE ITS RESEMBLANCE TO THAT FAMILY, THIS IS NOT AN ANEMONE. LIVING IN CORAL CREVICES OR SAND, IT COMES OUT AT NIGHT TO FEED, EXTENDING ITS TRANSLUCENT POLYPS WITH THEIR BALL-LIKE TIPS. IT QUICKLY RETRACTS THEM IF DISTURBED.

18

19

20

18   A SEA-SLUG, *HERMISSENDA CRASSICORNIS*, ON AN ANEMONE
(Richard Herrmann)
SEA-SLUGS, OR NUDIBRANCHS, ARE UNSHELLED MARINE SNAILS. THERE ARE A
LARGE NUMBER OF SPECIES – FOR EXAMPLE, OVER 400 OF THE *CHROMODORIS*
NUDIBRANCHS EXIST IN THE INDIAN AND PACIFIC OCEANS. EACH SPECIES HAS A
DISTINCTIVE BRIGHT COLOURING.

19   A *NEMBROTHA CRISTATA* ON CORAL, BORNEO
(Linda Pitkin)
SEA-SLUGS OCCUR IN TROPICAL OCEANS ALL OVER THE WORLD, IN SHALLOW
WATERS AROUND CORAL REEFS. THIS ONE APPEARS TO FEED ON SEA-SQUIRTS,
AND PRODUCES A TOXIN WHICH MAKES IT REPUGNANT TO MOST PREDATORS. ITS
VIVID COLORATION MAY SERVE TO WARN OF ITS POISONOUS NATURE.

20   A SPANISH SHAWL SEA-SLUG
(Norbert Wu)
AS WELL AS SEA-SQUIRTS, SEA-SLUGS FEED MAINLY ON ANEMONES, SPONGES AND
HORNY CORALS. OFTEN THEIR FOOD IS TOXIC, AND MANY SEA-SLUGS
INCORPORATE THE TOXINS FROM THEIR PREY INTO THEIR OWN TENTACLE-LIKE
FEATHERY OUTGROWTHS – WHICH FUNCTION LIKE GILLS – AND USE THEM FOR
DEFENCE. ALTERNATIVELY, TOXINS ARE SOMETIMES STORED IN WHITISH BUMPS
ON THE ANIMALS' SKIN. MOST SEA-SLUGS ARE SMALL, BUT ON AUSTRALIA'S
BARRIER REEF ONE SPECIES REACHES 30 CM (12 IN).

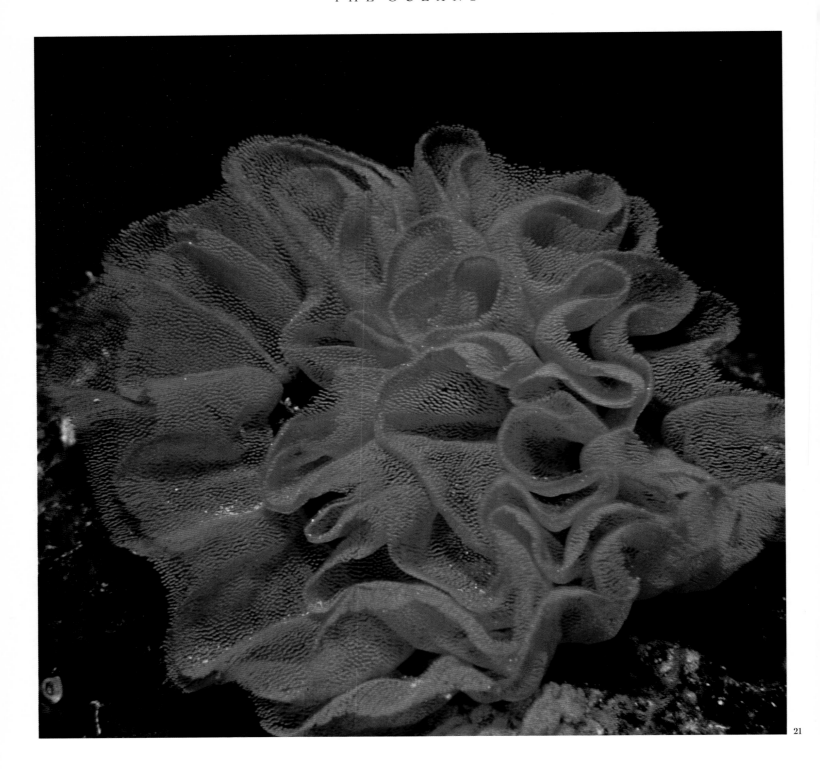

21

21   A SEA-SLUG EGG RIBBON, SOLOMON ISLANDS

(B. Jones & M. Shimlock)

THE SPAWNING MASS OF THE SPANISH DANCER SEA-SLUG, FOUND THROUGHOUT
THE INDO-PACIFIC REGION. SEA-SLUGS LAY EGG RIBBONS OF THE SAME COLOUR
AS THEIR OWN DOMINANT COLOUR, USUALLY SPIRALLED AROUND THEIR
FAVOURITE FOOD. SOME MASSES CAN CONTAIN A MILLION EGGS.

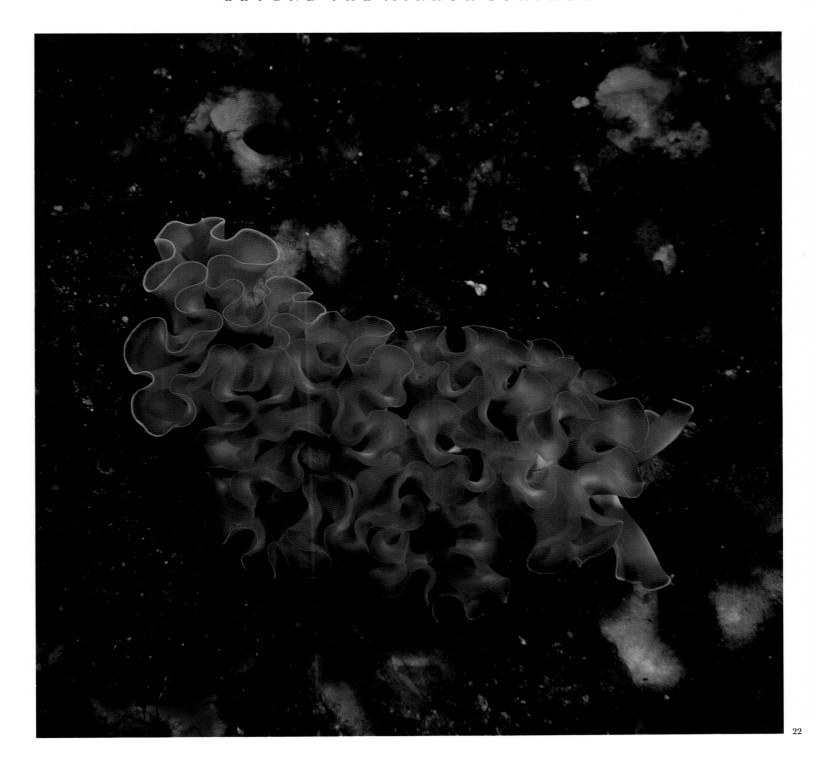

22

22   A LETTUCE SEA-SLUG, GRAND CAYMAN
(J. Michael Kelly)
THE NUMEROUS RUFFLES ON ITS BACK HAVE EARNED THIS NUDIBRANCH THE
NAME OF 'LETTUCE SEA-SLUG'. COMMON IN THE CARIBBEAN, FLORIDA AND THE
BAHAMAS, THE SPECIES SPORTS VARIOUS SHADES OF GREEN AND THE
OCCASIONAL BLUE, AND SOMETIMES HAS YELLOW OR RED MARKINGS.

23

24

25

23   A SLATE PENCIL URCHIN, HAWAII

(Norbert Wu)

THIS RARE SEA URCHIN IS EQUIPPED WITH THICK, STRONG, HOLLOW SPINES
WHICH GROW UP TO 13 CM (5 IN) LONG AND ARE VALUED AS BEADS.

24   A RADIANT STAR URCHIN, PAPUA NEW GUINEA

(David Hall)

ANOTHER OF THE LESS COMMON URCHINS, THE RADIANT STAR LIVES IN
SHALLOW WATER AMONGST SEAGRASS BEDS, WHERE IT SUSTAINS ITSELF ON
DEBRIS. UP TO 20 CM (8 IN) ACROSS, IT HAS HIGHLY VENOMOUS SPINES.

25   A FIRE SEA URCHIN, PHILIPPINES

(Norbert Wu)

THE BRILLIANT COLOURS OF THE FIRE SEA URCHIN INDICATE ITS POISONOUS
NATURE. MOST SPECIES OF SEA URCHIN HAVE BOTH LONG AND SHORT SPINES,
AMONG WHICH ARE TO BE FOUND THE LONG, SLENDER TUBE FEET. THE SPINES
ARE MOVABLE, AND AS WELL AS BEING USED FOR PROTECTION, THEY MAY ALSO
SERVE AS LEVERS, HELPING THE TUBE FEET IN LOCOMOTION. A FEW LONG-
SPINED TROPICAL KINDS WALK NOT ON TUBE FEET AT ALL, BUT ON THE TIPS OF
THEIR SPINES. AND SOME URCHINS USE THEIR SPINES, ALONG WITH THEIR TEETH,
TO BURROW INTO HARD ROCK.

CHAPTER TWO

THE BEAUTIFUL AND THE BIZARRE:
AN UNPARALLELED DIVERSITY
DR TUNDI AGARDY

The oceans cover two thirds of our planet's surface. In terms of sheer volume, they provide a greater range of living conditions than any other environment. Furthermore, life began to evolve in the seas many millions of years before any creature ventured on to dry land. Thus the scene was set for life to develop in the oceans in immense and extraordinary variety: creatures magnificent and monstrous, beautiful and bizarre.

HIGH NOON ON THE HIGH SEAS. FIVE HUNDRED KILO-metres (about 300 miles) from the nearest landmass, the jagged ocean surface suggests unbounded energy, unending motion. Standing waves, translucent grey-green walls of water, are internally propelled towards some distant shore. Over 500 million cubic km (120,000,000 cubic miles) of water are contained in the earth's seas, every molecule moving. There is something undeniably awe-inspiring about this vast, dynamic environment – something which perhaps reminds us, in a primitive, unquantifiable way, of our own evolutionary debt to the sea.

It is a debt shared by all of earth's creatures. Three and a half billion years ago, the primordial oceans spawned the first living organisms, and primitive marine creatures such as sponges, corals and jellyfish flourished for hundreds of millions of years before the invertebrates appeared and began their conquest of dry land. The sea has been the site of experiments in nature for far longer than any other environment, and this has helped to produce an extraordinary variety of marine life: a biological

---

26 BLUE MAOMAO, WITH A STARFISH AND SEA URCHINS
(Kim Westerskov)
THE SEA CONTAINS MANY BASIC LIFE FORMS FOUND NOWHERE ELSE. ONE SUCH IS A VAST GROUP CALLED ECHINODERMS, A PHYLUM OF GREAT AGE AND WORLDWIDE DISTRIBUTION, WHICH INCLUDES SEA URCHINS, STARFISH, BRITTLE-STARS AND SEA CUCUMBERS. THEY HAVE NO HEAD OR TAIL, BUT SHARE A FUNDAMENTAL SYMMETRY.

35

diversity which is without parallel on land. Whereas only one of the world's thirty-three basic animal life forms, or phyla, is exclusively terrestrial, fifteen are found only in the sea. Consider that phyla subdivide into classes, and thence to orders, families and genera before dividing into species – and you have some indication of the enormous range of life which exists in the ocean realms.

Why is the sea so hospitable to life? As land-living, air-breathing creatures we find it hard to comprehend. But sea-water is perhaps the best living medium there is, holding in readily available liquid solution the resources and chemicals which make life possible. Its heat-storing properties make it a buffer against the variable climate above, and its buoyancy has allowed unconventional physical forms to evolve, heedless of the constraints imposed by gravity.

Paradoxically, though, the marine environment also presents many obstacles to survival. The vastness of the ocean and the sheer power of its movements make it hard for any living thing to be in the right place at the right time. In a constantly changing world, chance plays a big role in survival. Moreover, from surface to seabed, from coast to open ocean, from pole through equator to pole, the sea encompasses an enormous range of environments with endless permutations of light, temperature, movement and availability of nutrients.

Consider, for example, the different set of living conditions present at each layer of the ocean. Near the surface, where upper ocean currents meander towards one another, collide, and veer off again, a thin stretch of sargassum and other weeds collects in a convergence zone. If we look carefully among the floating weed, a bustling and gloriously diverse little community is exposed. Minute copepods and other crustaceans, small fishes, carnivorous comb-jellies, jellyfish, the larvae and fry of coastal fish, even tiny hatchling sea turtles make the rich weed belt their home. Some are temporary visitors, using the weed lines as a nursery, while others stay for their entire lives.

Sunlight penetrates the top hundred metres (330 ft) of the sea, which is called the photic zone. Here, the microscopic algae collectively known as phytoplankton provide the basis for a huge, hungry food chain. Phytoplankton are food, in turn, for zooplankton – small creatures which also live in the photic zone, drifting with the upper currents. These plant and animal plankton are the staple diet of filter-feeding fish and mammals, including the blue whale – the largest mammal on earth.

Travelling down from the surface, we encounter blooms of single-celled and yellow-brown algae; flat, oval crustaceans known as isopods; more tiny free-living copepods, including shrimp-like crustaceans; moon-jellies, and more jellyfish. Here, too, synchronized schools of hunting fish – mackerel, bonito, or young albacore – sweep like silent amorphous ghosts in and out of view. Occasionally, a lone predatory white marlin or mako shark follows in their wake.

Some light even penetrates below the photic zone, to 200-metre (660-ft) depths, casting thick shafts of sunshine which give the water a sacred, ethereal look. But even further down, where the light shafts end in sword-like points and the water turns an ominous blue-black, midwater fishes swim and rest, swim and rest. Some of these species migrate towards the surface to feed during the safety of night, plunging back downwards at the first signs of daylight. Eels journeying from distant river mouths pass by, on their way to the mid-ocean spawning grounds where they will reproduce and then die. Giant shadows are cast when a hunting sperm whale dives into the depths, scattering fish in its wake. Hidden by the darkness, a giant squid flees, propelling itself further downwards.

Below three km (about 2 miles), the so-called abyssal depths are still teeming with thousands of species, each adapted in various ways to the rigours of living without light. Bizarre-looking flashlight fish blink signals to each other through the ink-dark water. An eerie glowing thunderhead formation in the distance reveals itself as a dense congregation of jellyfish, each emitting the cold light known as bioluminescence. Torpedo-shaped leatherback sea turtles that can weigh a thousand kg (2,200 lb) search the depths for such jellyfish, on which they feed.

Even five km (3 miles) down on the pockmarked seabed, life is on the move. Deep-sea creatures, able to survive in darkness and cold, and under immense pressure, await nourishment in the form of dead things drifting down from above. Fish, clams, worms and starfish have been found at up to ten-km (6-mile) depths on the ocean floor.

The ocean thus encourages life in a general sense, but each part of the environment challenges survival in innumerable specific ways. Besides the different levels of the ocean, there are many species-rich coastal habitats – mangroves and mudflats, rocky temperate coastlines, kelp forests, seagrass meadows, and of course coral reefs. Like all marine systems, each supports a highly specialized community of plants and animals, uniquely evolved to deal with the problems of that particular habitat. It is this range of living conditions in the context of a generally welcoming environment that sets the stage for biological diversity. As life forms evolve to become increasingly successful at dealing with ever more precise conditions, new species emerge – leading to the profusion of highly specialized marine forms we know today.

Time, too, is a factor. At work in the seas for three and a half billion years, evolution has produced some extraordinary creatures: jawless fishes, scorpion-like eurypterids, carrion-feeding cone-shelled nautiloids, enormous marine reptiles and giant squid. Some of the strangest variations are now extinct, but many species alive today have been present in the oceans for hundreds of millions of years – and many will probably survive for hundreds of millions more.

The true extent of marine diversity continues to elude us, however. Even close to shore, in waters that we mistakenly believe to be well studied and familiar, mysteries abound. As to the wider seas, and particularly their deepest levels, we know precious little of what is out there. Estimates of the total number of species of ocean fish, for example, range from 15,000 to over 40,000, with the figure of 25,000 most often cited. Confusion arises because some species have not yet been named, and others are named more than once because they vary so much from region to region, male to female. It is thought that up to a million undescribed species exist on the deep sea floor alone, to say nothing of the sombre intricacies of north Pacific kelp beds, which are the most productive of known habitats.

There are even unknown creatures among the rainbow denizens of the much loved, much studied coral reefs – but these may disappear before they have even been identified. Coral reefs are delicate, highly specialized systems, extremely sensitive to environmental change and disturbance. Tourist activities such as diving, fishing and glass-bottomed boating are taking their toll on reefs the world over. The effects of these pursuits are being exacerbated by more general problems such as pollution and increasing temperatures, which are acting to reduce genetic and species diversity before our very eyes.

It is perhaps tempting to compartmentalize the seas, to rank one area over another because it has more species, more unique features, or is simply more appealing. We sometimes speak of marine systems such as coral reefs or mangrove forests as though they were the separate rooms of a living museum: static, immutable and self-sufficient. We are wrong to do so.

The great web of life is nowhere so strongly unified as in the oceans: all habitats, and their communities, are ultimately linked. Changes occurring in one corner of the marine realm make far-reaching ripples. As we survey the unfathomable and mysterious ocean from our comfortable shores, we would do well to remember that we terrestrial beings are also influenced and nourished by the sea in ways that we are only just beginning to understand.

27   A BLUE SHARK WITH MACKEREL, UNDER DRIFTING KELP, CALIFORNIA
(Richard Herrmann)
AN OPEN-OCEAN PREDATOR, THE BLUE SHARK WILL DEVOUR ALMOST ANYTHING – INCLUDING MACKEREL. IT IS THE MOST ABUNDANT OF THE 350 KNOWN SHARK SPECIES, AND CAN BE FOUND IN ALL THE WORLD'S OCEANS. LARGE NUMBERS ARE OFTEN SEEN TOGETHER. ITS DOMINANCE MAY BE DUE TO ITS FLEXIBLE EATING HABITS AND NUMEROUS OFFSPRING: FEMALES MAY PRODUCE UP TO 130 YOUNG, WHICH IS FAR MORE THAN USUAL FOR SHARKS.

28   FAIRY BASSLETS AND PULLERS OVER A CORAL REEF, INDONESIA
(Linda Pitkin)
BASSLETS AND PULLERS ARE AMONGST THE MOST COMMON OF CORAL REEF
FISH. THEY TRAVEL IN LARGE SCHOOLS, STAYING CLOSE TO THE SAFETY OF
THE REEF AND FEEDING ON PLANKTON. AT NIGHT THEY RETREAT DEEP INTO
THE CORAL TO SLEEP. WHEN THEY SENSE DANGER, THE WHOLE SCHOOL
DARTS FOR COVER IN UNISON.

29

29   A SPINY BALLOONFISH, GRAND CAYMAN

(J. Michael Kelly)

ONE OF THE PUFFERFISH FAMILY, THE SPINY BALLOONFISH SWIMS SLOWLY NEAR
THE BOTTOM OF SEAGRASS MEADOWS, MANGROVE POOLS AND REEFS, WHERE ITS
COLOURING BLENDS WITH THE SURROUNDINGS. THESE FISH ARE OCCASIONALLY
ENCOUNTERED IN SMALL SCHOOLS. THE DISTINCTIVE LONG SPINES ARE USUALLY
LOWERED, BUT MAY BECOME ERECT EVEN WHEN THE BALLOONFISH IS NOT
INFLATED. AS A DEFENCE WHEN THREATENED, PUFFERFISH INGEST WATER AND
SWELL TO TWICE THEIR SIZE, TO GIVE A MORE FRIGHTENING APPEARANCE. IN
ADDITION, THEY STORE A DEADLY POISON, TETRAODOTOXIN, IN THEIR GONADS
AND LIVER. PREDATORS ARE FEW. SOME SPECIES ADVERTISE THEIR
VENOMOUSNESS WITH BRILLIANT WARNING COLOURS. IN JAPAN PUFFERFISH IS A
DELICACY, BUT EVEN A TRACE OF POISON CAN KILL; SEVERAL PEOPLE DIE EVERY
YEAR AS A RESULT.

30

**30   A GUINEAFOWL PUFFERFISH,
HAWAII**

(Norbert Wu)

PUFFERFISH HAVE STRONG, BEAK-
LIKE MOUTHS AND FEED ON HARD-
SHELLED ANIMALS SUCH AS SEA-
URCHINS, MOLLUSCS AND CRABS;
SMALL AMOUNTS OF SEAWEED ARE
ALSO FOUND IN THEIR STOMACHS.

31   A WOLF EEL, CALIFORNIA

(Norbert Wu)

BOTH ITS FEARSOME APPEARANCE
AND ITS NAME BELIE THE SHY
NATURE OF THE GIANT WOLF EEL,
WHICH MAY GROW TO OVER 2
METRES (6.5 FT) LONG. MALES AND
FEMALES FORM LIFELONG PAIRS
AND LIVE IN A SINGLE DEN. THE
WOLF EEL IS ONE OF THE FEW
CREATURES EQUIPPED TO EAT
SPINY SEA-URCHINS: IT HAS
POWERFUL JAWS, A STRONG SET OF
CANINE TEETH TO THE FRONT AND
A DOUBLE SET OF MOLARS AT THE
BACK.

31

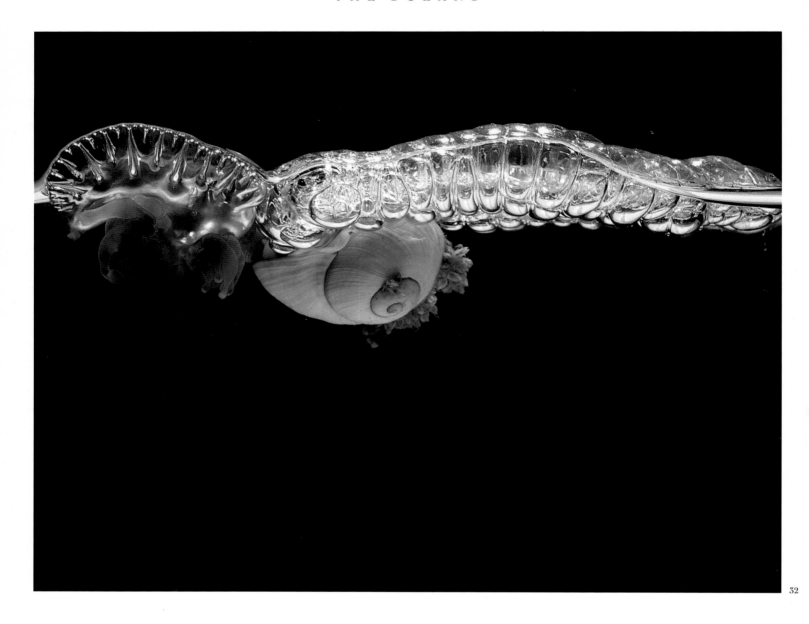

32

33

34

32 and 34   A SEA-SNAIL EATING A PORTUGUESE MAN-O'-WAR
(David Maitland/Planet Earth), **AND ANOTHER FEEDING ON A BY-THE-WIND SAILOR**
(David Maitland/Planet Earth)
THIS SURFACE-DWELLING SNAIL, MEASURING ABOUT A CENTIMETRE (.4 IN)
ACROSS ITS SHELL, SUSPENDS ITSELF UPSIDE DOWN FROM THE SEA'S SURFACE BY
CREATING A FLOATING RAFT OF BUBBLES WITH ITS FOOT.

33   A *GLAUCUS* SEA-SLUG DEVOURING A BY-THE-WIND SAILOR, ATLANTIC
(Peter Parks/Norbert Wu Photography)
AT THE SURFACE OF TROPICAL AND SUB-TROPICAL OPEN OCEAN DWELLS A
COMMUNITY OF ANIMALS CALLED THE 'PLEUSTON', OR 'BLUE COMMUNITY'
(BECAUSE OF ITS PREDOMINANTLY BLUE-MAUVE COLOURING). THE SEA-SLUG
SHOWN HERE HAS A BELLY FULL OF SWALLOWED AIR, WHICH CAUSES IT TO
FLOAT UPSIDE DOWN. THIS SEA-SLUG SPECIES HABITUALLY EATS THE STINGING
TENTACLES OF THE PORTUGUESE MAN-O'-WAR, AND INCORPORATES THE
STINGING TOXINS INTO ITS 'WINGS' FOR ITS OWN DEFENCE. HERE IT IS EATING A
BY-THE-WIND SAILOR, OR *VELELLA*, ANOTHER SURFACE DWELLER, WHOSE FLOAT
IS FULL OF CARBON MONOXIDE.

35

35   A JELLYFISH WITH A PACIFIC BUTTERFLY FISH, CALIFORNIA
(Richard Herrmann)
THE STINGING TENTACLES OF JELLYFISH ARE LETHAL TO MOST FISH, BUT
CERTAIN SPECIES HAVE EVOLVED PARTNERSHIPS WITH PARTICULAR JELLYFISH,
ENABLING THEM TO LIVE UNHARMED AMONG THE TENTACLES. THE PACIFIC
BUTTERFLY FISH, THE COMMENSAL PARTNER OF THIS *PELAGIA COLORATA*
JELLYFISH, GAINS PROTECTION FROM THE TENTACLES, BUT THE JELLYFISH DOES
NOT BENEFIT FROM THE RELATIONSHIP.

36

36 A PEDERSON CLEANER SHRIMP ON A NASSAU GROUPER, GRAND CAYMAN
(J. Michael Kelly)
SOME SHRIMPS FEED ON FISH MUCUS, REMOVING PARASITES AND BACTERIA
FROM THE FISH IN THE PROCESS. THIS 'CLEANER' SHRIMP IS COMMON
THROUGHOUT THE CARIBBEAN, WHERE IT LIVES IN ANEMONES. IN ORDER TO
ATTRACT FISH TO ITS 'CLEANING STATION', IT SITS ON THE ANEMONE, SWAYING
AND WAVING ITS ANTENNAE. FROM ITS PERCH, THE SHRIMP WILL 'SERVICE' A
SUCCESSION OF DIFFERENT FISH, NIBBLING OVER THEIR BODIES IN TURN – IT
WILL EVEN, IF APPROACHED SLOWLY, ATTEMPT TO CLEAN A DIVER'S FINGERS.
THIS ONE, SO TRANSPARENT THAT IT IS BARELY VISIBLE, IS CLEANING THE
GROUPER'S EYE.

37 A *PHYSOPHORA HYDROSTATICA*,
SARGASSO SEA
(Heather Angel)
SIPHONOPHORES, WHICH INCLUDE
THE PORTUGUESE MAN-O'-WAR,
MAKE USE OF THEIR GAS-FILLED
FLOATS TO CONTROL THEIR
BUOYANCY. THIS ONE PROPELS
ITSELF ALONG BY PULSING AND
SQUIRTING WATER THROUGH ITS
BELL-LIKE STRUCTURES. AN ACTIVE
CARNIVORE, IT DETECTS PREY
CHEMICALLY AND BY VIBRATIONS,
THEN ATTACKS WITH ITS
TENTACLES.

37

38   A LION'S MANE JELLYFISH, NEW ZEALAND

(David Hall)

THE WORLD'S LARGEST JELLYFISH, NAMED FOR ITS MASS OF 800 OR SO STINGING TENTACLES AND ITS TAWNY BELL. IN POLAR WATERS IT MAY REACH A METRE (OVER 3 FT) ACROSS, WITH FINGER-THICK TENTACLES TRAILING 10 METRES (33 FT) BEHIND IT. IT IS SAID TO FEEL OUT UNWARY DIVERS AS POTENTIAL PREY. SURPRISINGLY, WHITING LARVAE LIVE SAFELY AMONG THE TENTACLES, GAINING PROTECTION FROM PREDATORS.

38

39   AN OCTOPUS

(Norbert Wu)

THESE SHELL-LESS MOLLUSCS ARE
MAINLY BOTTOM-DWELLERS, IN
WARM TO TEMPERATE WATERS.
THEY LIVE SOLITARY LIVES AMONG
ROCKS OR IN HOLES. THEIR BAG-
LIKE BODIES CONCEAL A SHARP
BEAK, AND THEIR EIGHT MUSCULAR
ARMS ARE EQUIPPED WITH ROWS
OF SUCKERS. THEY LOCATE THEIR
PREY – CRUSTACEANS OR
PLANKTON – WITH THEIR VERY
SHARP EYES. OCTOPUSES CAN
BLEND WITH ALMOST ANY
BACKGROUND: SMALL BAGS OF
PIGMENT IN THEIR SKINS CAN
CONTRACT TO MAKE THE ANIMAL
ALMOST WHITE, OR EXPAND TO
MAKE IT DARK. IN THE GIANT
OCTOPUS THE USUAL DULL
COLOURING CAN CHANGE TO A
ROSY HUE, AS HERE.

39

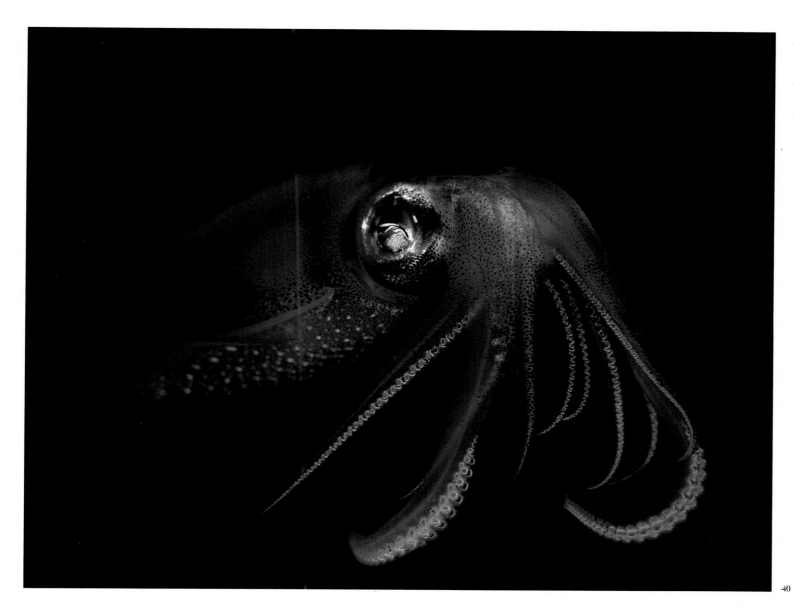

40

40 A CARIBBEAN REEF SQUID AT NIGHT

(J. Michael Kelly)

THE ONLY SQUID COMMON OVER CARIBBEAN REEFS. SQUID SWIM QUICKLY IN LARGE SCHOOLS, BY JET PROPULSION. THEY HAVE A WELL DEVELOPED SENSORY SYSTEM AND EXCEPTIONALLY GOOD EYE-TO-ARM COORDINATION. THE UNDERSIDES OF THE SQUID'S ARMS ARE COVERED WITH SUCTION DISCS; WITH THE TWO MUCH LONGER ARMS IT CAPTURES CRUSTACEANS AND FISH, WHICH IT TEARS APART WITH BEAKY JAWS.

41

41 A VENOMOUS SEA-SNAKE, PHILIPPINES

(David Hall)

FOUND AMONG CORAL REEFS IN THE INDO-PACIFIC AND IN OTHER ISOLATED AREAS, THIS SEA-SNAKE IS EXTREMELY POISONOUS, ITS VENOM CLOSELY RESEMBLING THAT OF ITS DISTANT RELATIVE THE COBRA. THE FAMILY TO WHICH IT BELONGS CONTAINS THE ONLY REPTILES TO BEAR LIVE YOUNG RATHER THAN LAYING EGGS. IT IS ALSO THE ONLY EXCLUSIVELY MARINE REPTILE, NOT EVEN VISITING LAND TO MATE OR GIVE BIRTH. NONETHELESS IT MUST BREATHE AIR, REMAINING SUBMERGED FOR NO MORE THAN 15 MINUTES AT A TIME.

42

42   A SAWFISH

(Norbert Wu)

LIKE SHARKS, SKATES AND RAYS, THE SAWFISH IS CARTILAGINOUS RATHER THAN
BONY. IT IS POSSIBLE THAT IT USES ITS SERRATED 'BEAK' FOR STUNNING OTHER
FISH AND HACKING THEM APART FOR EATING. THERE ARE 425 SPECIES OF SKATES,
RAYS AND SAWFISH.

43

43   A MANTA RAY, PHILIPPINES

(J. Michael Kelly)

THE GIANT MANTA RAY MAY WEIGH UP TO 2 TONNES, BUT IS HARMLESS DESPITE
ITS AWESOME APPEARANCE. THESE FISH ARE FOUND IN ALL THE WARM OCEANS
OF THE WORLD. UNLIKE MOST RAYS, MANTAS CRUISE NEAR THE SURFACE OF THE
OPEN SEA FEEDING ON PLANKTON, AND ARE SELDOM SEEN OVER REEFS. FROM
TIME TO TIME THEY LEAP CLEAR OF THE WATER, THEN COME CRASHING DOWN
AGAIN – THE REASON FOR THIS PERFORMANCE IS A MYSTERY, BUT IT MAY HELP
TO REMOVE IRRITATING PARASITES, OR IT MAY BE AN EXPRESSION OF THE
ANIMAL'S TERRITORIAL RIGHTS.

44

44   A MANATEE WITH YOUNG, FLORIDA

(Armin Maywald)

THESE SLOW-MOVING CREATURES INCLUDE SEVERAL SPECIES WHICH OCCUR IN
THE ESTUARIES AND COASTAL WATERS OF THE CARIBBEAN AND PARTS OF WEST
AFRICA. THE ONLY EXCLUSIVELY VEGETARIAN MARINE MAMMALS, THEY LIVE ON
VARIOUS SEAWEEDS, NEEDING ABOUT 90 KG (200 LB) A DAY IN ORDER TO
MAINTAIN BODY WEIGHT – WHICH MAY BE 800 KG (1,760 LB). MANATEES ARE
USUALLY 2.5 TO 4.5 METRES (8-15 FT) LONG. THEIR SLUGGISHNESS, POOR SIGHT
AND SENSE OF SMELL MAKE THEM VERY VULNERABLE. THEY ARE ALSO UNDER
THREAT FROM POLLUTION, DESTRUCTION OF HABITAT AND DAMAGE BY
OUTBOARD MOTORS AND FISHING NETS, THOUGH IN SOME AREAS THEY ARE NOW
PROTECTED.

45   GREEN TURTLES MATING, KALIMANTAN, INDONESIA

(B. Jones & M. Shimlock)

GREEN TURTLES ARE FOUND IN MOST TEMPERATE OCEANS, AND FEED ON SEA-
GRASS AND ALGAE. THESE TWO WEIGH 75-100 KG (165-220 LB). MATING TAKES PLACE
THOUSANDS OF MILES AWAY FROM THE TURTLES' FEEDING GROUNDS. WHEN THE
FEMALE DEPOSITS HER HUNDRED OR SO SOFT WHITE EGGS, IT WILL BE ON THE
VERY BEACH WHERE SHE HERSELF HATCHED. LIKE ALL MARINE TURTLE SPECIES,
GREENS ARE ENDANGERED – HUNTING BY HUMANS, THE COLLECTING OF THEIR
EGGS, AND 'DEVELOPMENT' OF THEIR HATCHING BEACHES ARE THEIR GREATEST
HAZARDS.

45

46

**46   A HAMMERHEAD SHARK,
GALAPAGOS ISLANDS**
(Paul Humann/Jeff Rotman Photography)
THE COMMON HAMMERHEAD
GROWS TO A LENGTH OF 4 METRES
(13 FT) OR MORE. THE T-SHAPED
HEAD, WHICH HAS AN EYE AND A
NOSTRIL AT EACH END OF THE T,
SWINGS FROM SIDE TO SIDE AS THE
SHARK HUNTS – FOR OTHER
SHARKS, RAYS AND SKATES. THEY
ARE SOMETIMES FISHED FOR THEIR
SKIN AND OIL.

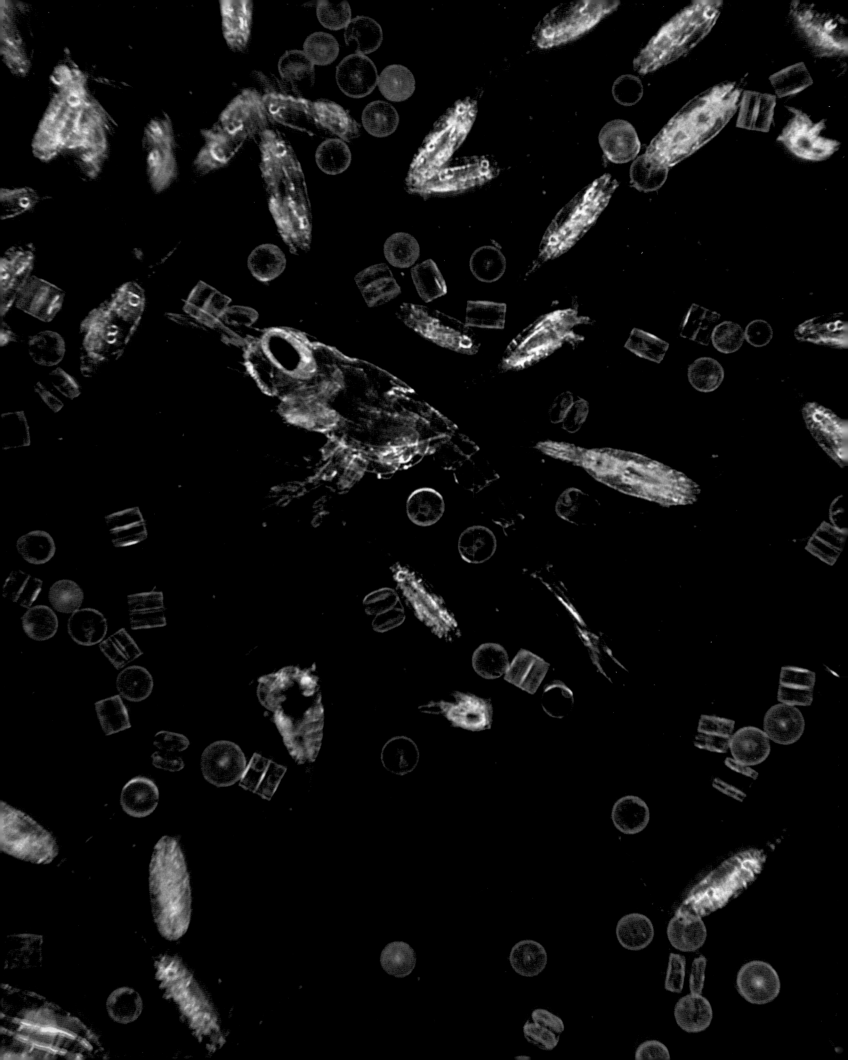

CHAPTER THREE

THE PLANKTON POWERHOUSE:
ENERGY CAPTURE IN THE SEA
Dr Ian Joint

Every one of the ocean's creatures, from the tiniest shrimp to the great blue whale, depends for its survival on some of the smallest organisms on earth: the single-celled marine algae known as phytoplankton. Their growth varies enormously with time and place, according to the great cycles of earth, water and atmosphere, and profoundly influences the nature of every marine habitat.

To the casual observer, the blue waters of the oceans appear largely devoid of plant life. A drifting clump of seaweed, or perhaps a stretch of seagrass, are the only obvious forms of vegetation. But examine a drop of sea-water under a microscope, and it tells a very different story. A myriad organisms are revealed: some resemble spheres, cups, hooks or stars, and bear flagella, little whip-like appendages which allow motility; others, the diatoms, have hard cell walls constructed from silica in diverse and strangely beautiful forms.

These are the phytoplankton: single-celled marine plants which are present in their masses over vast stretches of the ocean, and on which all marine life ultimately depends.

The term *plankton* comes from a Greek word meaning 'wanderer'. Plankton have little control over their movements but are swept through the oceans at the mercy of currents and tides. Most phytoplankton measure less than a fiftieth of a millimetre (0.008 in) across; indeed, some species are no more than a thousandth of a millimetre (0.00004 in). Yet these microscopic organisms have one all-important attribute: the ability to photosynthesize.

Photosynthesis is the basis of all life in the seas and on land. Plants – whether ocean plankton or our familiar trees and grasses – have evolved complex mechanisms enabling them to capture the energy present in sunlight. Using this energy, they convert atmospheric carbon dioxide into new biomass, or organic matter. Just as photosynthesis by terrestrial plants produces the materials which ultimately feed every land-living animal, so plankton, 'the grass of the oceans', directly or indirectly support every one of the sea's creatures.

However, photosynthesis can take place only in the thin uppermost layer of the water which is illuminated by sunlight. It is brightest above 100 metres (330 ft), and below about 200, all light disappears. At the surface the phytoplankton feast on light and multiply, capturing the energy which powers the entire ocean ecosystem. Given the right conditions, phytoplankton can increase by 300 per cent in a single day; a cubic metre (35 cubic ft) of ocean water may contain 700,000 plants.

Where phytoplankton bloom, an assortment of marine animals known as zooplankton follow. These range from the microscopically small to several centimetres in size. Some are herbivorous and others carnivorous; many are crustacean-like, but all show a great diversity in form. Some are the larvae of creatures such as lobsters, crabs and mussels, and will adopt a different lifestyle when they mature; others will float through the seas as plankton for their entire lives. The smaller, herbivorous organisms graze phytoplankton from the rich plant soup in which they swim; commonest are the shrimp-like copepods, which use their hairy legs to sweep plant cells into their mouths. Carnivorous forms include miniature jellyfish and elegant elongate arrow-worms, which dart at prey with formidable hooked jaws.

The zooplankton are themselves food for an enormous range of creatures, from the shrimps to the giant baleen whales. Between these two extremes are many other zooplankton-feeders: corals, sponges, sea-squirts and bivalve molluscs such as the familiar oysters and mussels. Ocean predators and scavengers of all kinds complete the marine food web. Ultimately, every one of these organisms depends on the phytoplankton. But why should plankton be abundant in some places and virtually non-existent in others? Contrast the crystal-clear waters where phytoplankton grow thinly with the rich blooms which appear in polar seas. What factors and processes are at work?

Plants derive their energy from sunlight. However, as every gardener knows, growing plants need not only light, but essential nutrients such as nitrates and phosphates. These are present in sea-water in limited quantities, but are quickly depleted by rapidly multiplying phytoplankton in the restricted sunlit zone. Deeper down, the sediment-laden waters hold fresh nutrients, but unless mixed into the surface, these are useless to the phytoplankton. The hotter the sun, the greater the problem, because heated sea-water loses density and tends to float above cooler water. The warmed surface waters become a distinct layer which cannot mix with the cold, nutrient-rich mass below.

To some extent this phenomenon occurs in oceans throughout the world, but different ecosystems are affected in different ways. In temperate regions, for example, the spring sunshine warms the winter-cold waters, but only to a depth of about 100 metres (330 ft). Phytoplankton quickly bloom in the increased sunlight, supplying food for the zooplankton, which in turn attract large fish and bird populations. By summer, however, the phytoplankton have often exhausted all the plant nutrients within their growing zone, and production tails off. But it does not cease completely; the animals which feed on the phytoplankton also excrete ammonia, a nutrient source which is scavenged by the plant cells to sustain growth throughout summer.

As autumn progresses, light levels diminish. The surface waters lose heat and are stirred by the winds and tides into the dark, cold water below. The phytoplankton are swept down too, and though the water surrounding them now holds nutrients in plenty, there is no sunlight available for photosynthesis. Plant production declines until the following spring when the waters are heated once more, and the oceanic production cycle begins anew.

In the Arctic and Antarctic seas, very different conditions prevail. Temperatures are below zero and there are long periods of perpetual darkness. However, when the long winter is over, nutrients are plentiful and the summer provides continuous light. Moreover, melting ice caps release fresh water into the ocean; this is less dense than the salty sea-water and so, as happens during the spring in temperate regions, one layer of water floats above the rest. This buoys the phytoplankton up into the sunlight; conditions are ideal for plant growth, and life rapidly burgeons.

During the brief Antarctic summer, the key role of phytoplankton in supporting other marine life is given clear and dramatic illustration. When sunlight illuminates the austere and icy seas, the diatoms are triggered into furious productivity. This sudden abundance of plant food supports a proliferation of zooplankton, especially the shrimp-like crustaceans known as krill. These animals form dense swarms in Antarctic waters which may be 10 metres (33 ft) deep and cover hundreds of square kilometres.

Huge numbers of penguins and the giant baleen whales feast on this plenty. Some whales migrate thousands of kilometres to the Antarctic to exploit this great resource. None is more impressive than the blue whale, which can devour up to three tonnes of krill per day. With an average weight of 150 tonnes and a length up to 27 metres (90 ft), these are the largest animals ever to have lived.

The short, three-tier Antarctic food web which maintains these magnificent creatures is typical of the polar seas. Light energy is captured by the diatoms, which are grazed by the krill, which in turn are eaten by penguins and whales. Because so few stages are involved, energy is transferred efficiently and quickly from very small organisms to some of the largest on earth.

In contrast, food webs in the tropical oceans are long and much less efficient, certainly in terms of supporting higher animals. The surface waters are permanently warm, rarely mixing with the deeper layers, and so tend to be poor in nutrients throughout the year. Exceptionally small phytoplankton – measuring only a thousandth of a millimetre (0.00004 in) – can best exploit such conditions, and dominate these waters. However, they sustain a very different food web from that of the Antarctic. Being too small for ordinary zooplankton to graze, they are consumed instead by protozoa, micro-organisms which are themselves no bigger than a tenth of a millimetre (0.004 in). Krill and copepods feed on the protozoa, but this extra level in the food web has an ecological cost. Since every plant and animal uses some energy simply to maintain its life processes, this energy is effectively lost to the ecosystem – and to the higher animals which might use it. Consequently tropical oceans, though diverse, rarely sustain the dense populations of large animals which are a feature of other seas.

Certain coastal regions, like the Chile-Peru coast of South America, are the exception. Here, deep, nutrient-rich water is brought to the surface by constant upwelling. Larger phytoplankton cells grow, zooplankton flourish, and the area teems with fish and birds, supported once again by a short food chain.

All life in the oceans depends, therefore, on phytoplankton as the primary food source, but the ideal combination of light and nutrients necessary for their growth occurs only at certain places, and at certain times. The vast ocean gyres north and south of the equator, for example, are marine deserts, their warm, beautiful, luminous blue waters virtually devoid of life. Yet even here, when unusual events bring nutrients welling to the surface, the few phytoplankton present quickly respond and plant life blooms.

And along those tropical coasts where upwelling is constant, and in the polar and temperate regions, masses of minute plant and animal organisms thrive and multiply, sustaining the life of the world's oceans in all its astonishing diversity of size, colour and form.

---

48 ATLANTIC PTEROPODS, OR SEA BUTTERFLIES

(Heather Angel)

THESE MINUTE MOLLUSCS (*DIACRIA MAJOR*), ACTIVE A HUNDRED METRES (330 FT) BELOW THE SURFACE OF THE SEA, ARE MUCUS WEB FEEDERS. THEY SPREAD A NET OF MUCUS AROUND THEMSELVES IN WHICH TO TRAP PHYTOPLANKTON. THEN THEY SUCK THE MUCUS BACK INTO THEIR BODIES, AND DIGEST THE PLANT CELLS.

49   THE GRASS OF THE OCEANS
(Harold Taylor/OSF)
PHYTOPLANKTON, LIKE GRASS ON LAND, ARE THE PRIMARY PRODUCERS OF THE
OCEAN. THEIR TINY CELLS CONTAIN CHLOROPHYLL, THE GREEN PIGMENT WHICH
ENABLES ALL PLANTS TO PHOTOSYNTHESIZE BY TRAPPING THE ENERGY OF
SUNLIGHT, TO FORM BIOMASS FROM CARBON DIOXIDE AND WATER.

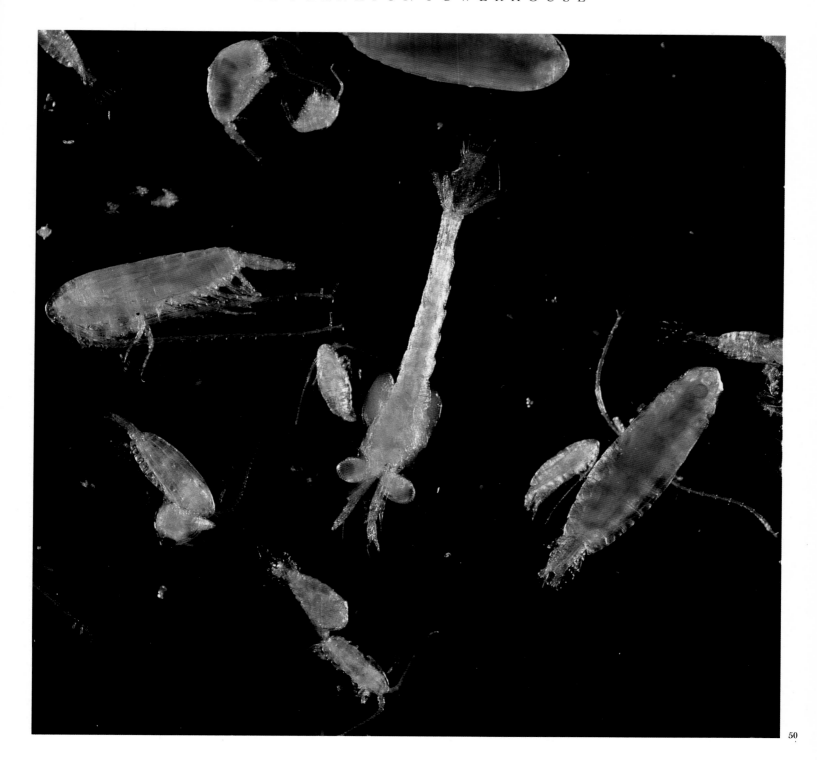

50

50   ASSORTED ANIMAL PLANKTON

(Harold Taylor/OSF)

'ZOOPLANKTON' IS A TERM THAT ENCOMPASSES ALL THE TINY ANIMALS THAT
FEED ON PHYTOPLANKTON, AND ON OTHER ANIMAL PLANKTON. THEY ARE
FOUND AT ALL DEPTHS, BUT ARE MORE NUMEROUS AT THE SURFACE, ESPECIALLY
AT NIGHT. MANY ARE LARVAL FORMS OF CRUSTACEANS, AND WILL EVOLVE INTO
VERY DIFFERENT-LOOKING CREATURES.

51

52

53

51   ATLANTIC KRILL

(Heather Angel)

KRILL ARE ONE OF THE MOST ABUNDANT KINDS OF ANIMAL PLANKTON, PRESENT THROUGHOUT THE WORLD'S OCEANS. DURING THE POLAR SUMMER, ANTARCTIC SPECIES GATHER IN MASSIVE SWARMS, TO BE FED ON BY SOME OF THE LARGEST MARINE CREATURES, INCLUDING BALEEN (FILTER-FEEDING) WHALES, AND PENGUINS.

52   AN AMPHIPOD, *THEMISTO COMPRESSA*

(Heather Angel)

FOUND IN THE NORTH ATLANTIC, THIS TINY CRUSTACEAN – ANOTHER KIND OF ZOOPLANKTON – IS NORMALLY A VORACIOUS CARNIVORE, BUT DURING THE SPRING IT ALSO FEEDS ON PLANT PLANKTON. THERE ARE ABOUT 3,600 SPECIES – FRESH-WATER AS WELL AS MARINE. AMPHIPODS ARE PARTICULARLY EFFICIENT SCAVENGERS.

53   A SHALLOW WATER HOPPER

(IOS)

A PREDATOR OF OTHER ANIMAL PLANKTON, THE WATER HOPPER IS ANOTHER CRUSTACEAN, LIVING AT THE OCEAN'S SURFACE. MOST PLANKTONIC ORGANISMS HAVE LITTLE OR NO POWER OF LOCOMOTION, AND MERELY DRIFT OR FLOAT, WHEREVER TIDE OR CURRENT TAKES THEM.

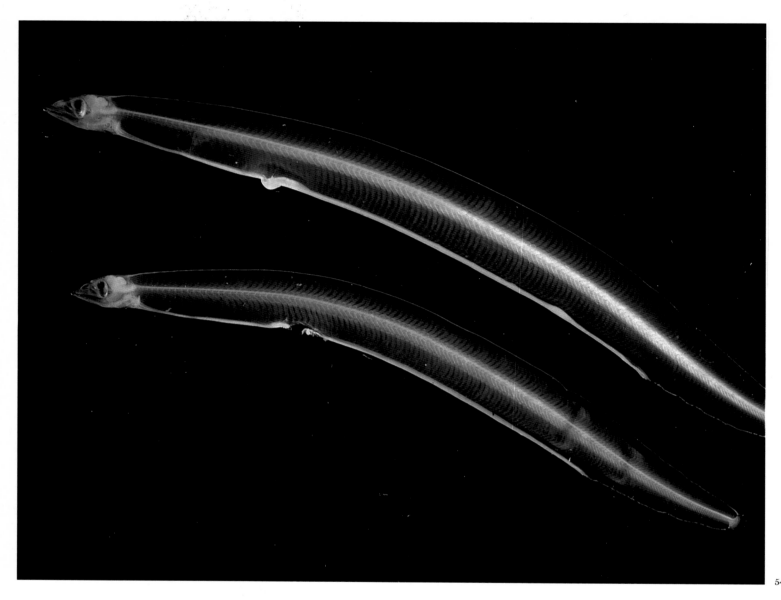

54

54 and 55   DEEP-SEA EEL LARVAE
(Heather Angel) **AND OTHER ANIMAL**
PLANKTON, BERMUDA
(Peter Parks/OSF)
LIKE MANY MARINE CREATURES,
EELS BEGIN THEIR LIVES AS
PLANKTONIC LARVAE, DRIFTING
WITH THE UPPER CURRENTS. THEIR
EXTREME TRANSPARENCY HELPS
TO CAMOUFLAGE THEM AGAINST
PREDATORS. ANIMAL PLANKTON
INCLUDE A VERY WIDE VARIETY OF
ORGANISMS – IN FACT, EVERY
ANIMAL PHYLUM IS REPRESENTED,
EVEN IF, AS WITH EEL LARVAE,
LIVING AS PLANKTON IS ONLY ONE
PHASE OF THEIR EXISTENCE.
ABOUT 70 PER CENT OF PLANKTON
ARE CRUSTACEANS, OF WHICH THE
PREDOMINANT CLASS IS THE
COPEPODS. IN ADDITION TO
COPEPODS, THE OTHER ANIMAL
PLANKTON SHOWN HERE INCLUDE

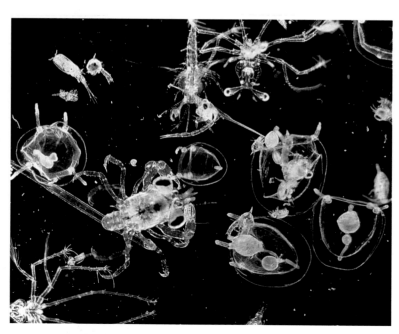

TINY JELLYFISH AND CRAB LARVAE.
UNLIKE CRABS AND EELS,
COPEPODS DO NOT MATURE INTO
DIFFERENT FORMS, BUT REMAIN
PLANKTON ALL THEIR LIVES.

55

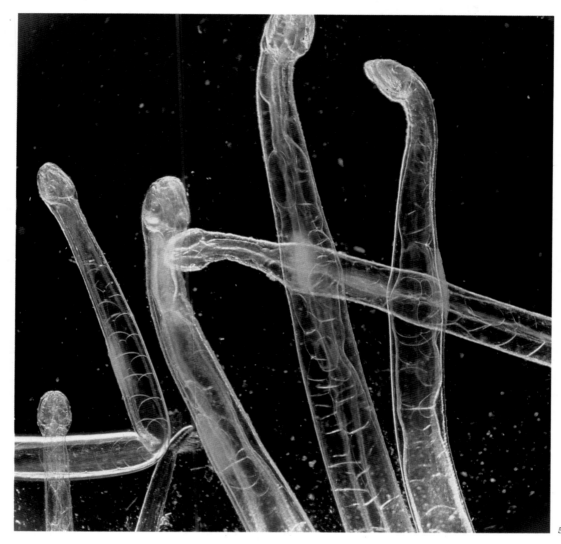

56

56   ARROW-WORMS
(Mike Laverack/Planet Earth)
SWARMING AMONGST PLANKTON, ARROW-WORMS ARE FEARSOME PREDATORS,
DEVOURING VAST QUANTITIES OF FISH EGGS – BUT THEY, IN TURN, ARE PREYED
UPON BY FISH. DIFFERENT SPECIES OF ARROW-WORMS ARE THE CLASSIC
'INDICATORS' FOR THE FISHERMEN OF SOUTHWEST ENGLAND: IN PAST DECADES
THE ABUNDANCE OF ONE SPECIES WAS LINKED TO THE PRESENCE OF HERRING,
BUT ANOTHER SPECIES WAS MOST ABUNDANT WHEN ANCHOVIES AND SARDINES
REPLACED THE HERRING.

57   A SEAL MOTHER AND HER PUP, SWIMMING

(Kim Westerskov)

IN MOST SEAL SPECIES THE FEMALES GIVE BIRTH A YEAR AFTER MATING, SO THAT THE YOUNG ARE BORN ON LAND, JUST BEFORE THE NEXT BREEDING SEASON. THE PUPS ARE NURSED WHILE ON LAND, USUALLY FOR SEVERAL MONTHS. MOST SPECIES HAVE ACUTE HEARING, AND SOME MAKE USE OF SONAR FOR UNDERWATER NAVIGATION.

57

58

58   A CRAB-EATER SEAL, SWIMMING UNDER ICE

(Paul Drummond/B. & C. Alexander)

ALTHOUGH MOST SEALS ARE MAINLY FISH-EATERS, SOME, SUCH AS THE MISLEADINGLY NAMED CRAB-EATER SEAL OF THE ANTARCTIC, FEED ON KRILL AND OTHER ANIMAL PLANKTON.

59   A HUMPBACK WHALE FEEDING ON KRILL, ANTARCTICA

(Peter Scoones/Planet Earth)

DESPITE THEIR ENORMOUS SIZE, BALEEN WHALES SUCH AS THE HUMPBACK LIVE
ON ANIMAL PLANKTON, ESPECIALLY KRILL – SOMETIMES CONSUMING SEVERAL
TONNES A DAY. SWIMMING WITH THEIR MOUTHS OPEN, THEY FILTER THE KRILL
BY TAKING LARGE GULPS OF SEA-WATER, THEN EXPELLING IT THROUGH THE
FRINGES OF BALEEN (WHALEBONE) WHICH LINE THEIR MOUTHS. BEHIND THE
BALEEN 'STRAINER' VAST AMOUNTS OF KRILL ARE CAUGHT, WHICH THE WHALES
THEN SWALLOW.

**60   BLACK-BROWED ALBATROSSES
FEEDING IN THE SOUTH ATLANTIC**
(Peter J. Oxford/Planet Earth)
THE ALBATROSSES SEEN HERE ARE
SCAVENGING IN THE WAKE OF A
FISHING TRAWLER. THEY TOO
USUALLY EAT KRILL, WHICH
ABOUND IN THESE WATERS DURING
THE SUMMER. THE ABSENCE OF
VERTEBRATE PREDATORS, AND
THEIR ADAPTATION TO LIFE AT SEA,
FIT THESE BIRDS PERFECTLY FOR
POLAR REGIONS, WHERE THEY
ESTABLISH COLONIES ON REMOTE
SUB-ANTARCTIC ISLANDS.

61

**61   GREGARIOUS CHINSTRAP PENGUINS RALLYING ON AN ICEBERG, DECEPTION
ISLAND, ANTARCTICA**

(Ben Osborne)

LIKE THE BALEEN WHALES, ANTARCTIC PENGUINS FEED AT SEA ON KRILL. (WHEN
ON LAND THEY EAT NOTHING, SUBSISTING ON THE LAYER OF FAT UNDER THEIR
SKINS.) EVER SINCE WHALE NUMBERS BEGAN TO DECLINE SO DRAMATICALLY,
THERE HAS BEEN MORE AND MORE FOOD AVAILABLE FOR THESE BIRDS, AND
THEIR POPULATIONS HAVE INCREASED – A CLEAR DEMONSTRATION OF THE
INFLUENCE THAT ONE ORGANISM HAS ON ANOTHER IN THE FOOD WEB. ON LAND
PENGUINS WADDLE AWKWARDLY ON THEIR TWO LEGS, BUT ARE AGILE AND
GRACEFUL IN THE WATER.

62

63

62   ADÉLIE PENGUINS DIVING FROM AN ICEBERG, ANTARCTICA

(Ben Osborne)

PENGUINS ARE SUPERB SWIMMERS AND DIVERS. THEY SWIM BY MEANS OF THEIR FLIPPER-LIKE WINGS, USING THEIR WEBBED FEET AS RUDDERS. THEY ARE HIGHLY SOCIAL CREATURES – AS MANY AS HALF A MILLION HAVE BEEN COUNTED IN ONE ANTARCTIC COLONY. ADÉLIE PENGUINS MAKE THEIR NESTS ON HIGH CLIFFS REACHED BY STEEP SLOPES, UP WHICH THEY MUST SLOWLY TOIL EACH TIME THEY RETURN FROM THE SEA – PERHAPS SEVERAL TIMES A DAY. BUT THEY HAVE NO DIFFICULTY WITH THE RETURN JOURNEY – THEY SIMPLY SKI DOWNHILL, OR TOBOGGAN DOWN ON THEIR FRONTS.

63   A PENGUIN AT A HOLE IN THE ICE

(Kim Westerskov)

PENGUINS CAN DIVE AS DEEP AS 200 METRES (660 FT), BUT MUST COME TO THE SURFACE TO BREATHE. UNDER WATER THEY CAN SWIM UP TO 40 KM (25 MILES) AN HOUR. THEIR STIFF FEATHERS, OILED AND WATERPROOF, SERVE AS INSULATION. THEIR CHIEF ENEMIES ARE THE KILLER WHALE, THE SKUA GULL AND THE LEOPARD SEAL. IN SHORT ENCOUNTERS THE PENGUIN CAN OUTSWIM THE SEAL AND ESCAPE BACK ON TO LAND, BUT IF THE PURSUIT IS EXTENDED, THE SEAL IS LIKELY TO CATCH IT.

64

64   A POLAR BEAR MOTHER WITH HER CUBS, CAPE CHURCHILL, CANADA
(Heather Angel)
AT THE TOP OF THE FOOD CHAIN, THESE LARGE CARNIVORES HAVE NO NATURAL
PREDATORS OTHER THAN HUMAN BEINGS. BUT LIKE ALL SEA CREATURES THEY
ARE ULTIMATELY RELIANT ON PLANT PLANKTON, WHICH PROVIDE FOOD FOR THE
KRILL WHICH IN TURN SUSTAIN THE FISH AND SEALS ON WHICH POLAR BEARS
PREY. POLAR BEARS USUALLY LIVE ON DRIFTING PACK ICE, BUT SOMETIMES
WANDER LONG DISTANCES INLAND. POWERFUL SWIMMERS, THEY MAY CROSS 50
KM (30 MILES) OF WATER AT A TIME.

65

65   A POLAR BEAR CUB, NORTH WEST TERRITORIES, CANADA
(Jim Brandenburg/Planet Earth)
THE PREGNANT POLAR BEAR MAKES A DEN IN THE SNOW, AND IN JANUARY GIVES
BIRTH TO TWO TINY, HELPLESS CUBS, WHICH SHE NURSES, STILL IN THE DEN,
UNTIL MARCH. THE CUBS REMAIN DEPENDENT ON HER FOR THE FIRST TWO AND
A HALF YEARS. THEY ADOPT THE FLEXIBLE EATING HABITS OF ADULTS, HUNTING
SEALS AND FISH AND SOMETIMES SEABIRDS, AND SCAVENGING FROM WHALE
CARCASSES. POLAR BEARS ARE QUITE FEARLESS, AND WILL STALK ANY ANIMALS,
INCLUDING HUMANS.

CHAPTER FOUR

PILOTS OF THE OPEN OCEAN:
THE GREAT MARINE MIGRATIONS

MARK SIMMONDS

The great rhythms of the world's oceans affect every creature inhabiting them. Every year, a multitude of fish and sea mammals are prompted by mysterious cues to embark on remarkable journeys across the seas in order to feed or breed. Many navigate thousands of kilometres of open ocean to precise locations, guided by sensory capabilities still only guessed at.

THE WESTERN ROCKS, A JAGGED CROWN OF ISLETS AT the south-westernmost point of the British Isles, mark the edge of the mighty Atlantic Ocean. The boatmen of the Isles of Scilly know these hostile waters well, and on calmer days will take more intrepid sightseers to view the Bishop Rock light-house. Even on such days, a powerful oceanic swell brings the sea crashing and foaming around the rocks. The ungainly tourist boats roll precariously in the water, under the curious gaze of scores of grey seals.

Maintaining their position at the surface with subtle, almost imperceptible movements of their flippers, the seals are supremely indifferent to the boiling frenzy around them. They, after all, are in their natural element. Their bodies and lifestyles have been shaped by the endless motion of the water and the in-cessant beat of the seasons: the massive ocean rhythms which govern the life of every one of the sea's creatures.

The world's oceans are driven by global winds and the move-ment of the planet itself into huge circulating water masses, or gyres, encompassing many thousands of kilometres. The great

---

66 A BLACK-BROWED ALBATROSS, DRAKE PASSAGE, SOUTH ATLANTIC
(Ben Osborne)
THIS IS PROBABLY THE COMMONEST OF THE ELEVEN SPECIES OF ALBATROSS AND,
LIKE ALL THE OTHERS, IT IS A SUPERB OCEAN FLIER. A VERY LONG BUT
RELATIVELY NARROW WING SHAPE ALLOWS THESE BIRDS TO EFFORTLESSLY
GLIDE OVER THE SEA FOR MONTHS, ONLY RETURNING TO LAND TO NEST AND
RAISE THEIR YOUNG.

subtropical gyres revolve anticyclonically around the ocean basins – clockwise in the north and anticlockwise in the south. North of these, other gyres rotate, and at the western margins of all these giant circulations intense and powerful currents are produced. The Gulf Stream is one such current, flowing as a broad, meandering band of warm water from the Florida coast across the Atlantic to heat the western coast of Scotland.

At the edges of these gyres and currents, variations in the climate and the contours of the ocean bed spawn smaller currents and eddies. Both the greater and the lesser water movements regulate productivity in the seas. In places where the huge wheels of the ocean mechanism conspire to bring deep, nutrient-rich water up into the light, plant plankton, the base of marine food webs, spasm into life.

The Antarctic divergence is one region where such upwelling occurs, and in the short polar summer this fuels tremendous productivity. Plant plankton bloom profusely and are devoured by swarms of shrimp-like krill. This seasonal plenty attracts a variety of fabulous creatures to the Antarctic waters every year, including the blue whales, which, incredibly, refuel their massive metabolisms with billions of tiny krill. Many of the great whales visit the rich feeding grounds of the Arctic and Antarctic during the polar summers. Their calves, however, need warmth, so most species breed and calve in the tropics. Their twice-yearly migrations from cold to warm waters and back cover thousands of kilometres, and may take several months to complete.

The grey whales of the northern hemisphere are unparalleled cetacean travellers, making the longest known annual migration of any mammal. In summer, grey whales feed in the shallow, food-rich Arctic waters of the Bering, Beaufort and Chukchi Seas. But with remarkably precise timing, as chill winds begin to whip across the ocean, thousands of greys abandon their feeding grounds and begin their journey towards the warm, protected lagoons of Baja California in Mexico. Pregnant females usually lead the migration, following a predetermined route that is learned by each new generation. Leaving through the Unimak Pass in the Aleutian Chain, they journey south along the continental shelf past southeast Alaska and British Columbia, and from there follow the shoreline to Mexico. Here, in the warm coastal waters, the females bear their young. The entire journey covers an extraordinary 11,000 km (nearly 7,000 miles).

Little or no food is consumed by the greys or the other great whales during these long months of migration and breeding. Instead they live off their rich stores of fibrous blubber – in some species over a third of a metre (1 ft) thick – accumulated during the weeks of summer feasting. Unfortunately, this vast energy store is also prized by human hunters for its high oil yield, with the result that many whale species are now poised on the brink of extinction.

Most of the smaller, toothed whales and dolphins are epic travellers too. Sometimes they follow schools of squid or fish, but at other times they are clearly responding to seasonal rhythms. On America's east coast, for example, bottlenose dolphins live off northerly New Jersey during summer; but they, like many Americans, prefer to winter nearer to Florida. Mysteriously, schools of hundreds, and sometimes thousands, of dolphins may form out at sea. Why this happens is unclear, but they are travelling, always travelling.

Certain seal species also make great ocean journeys. Grey seals travel in straight lines of almost mathematical precision for hundreds of kilometres to fish-rich feeding grounds. Harp seals, meanwhile, do not even visit land to breed. For just two weeks early in the year, thousands of females gather on the thin Arctic ice to bear their young. Afterwards, they briefly consort with the waiting males to secure next season's offspring, before setting off for their feeding grounds in Hudson and Baffin Bays. There the seals disperse until the following season, when they are once more called north to family life on a frozen sea.

Below the waves, there are legendary voyagers among the fish. Young salmon mature in their natal rivers and streams; but after a few years they don the silvery camouflage of seafish and head in their millions for the open sea, where they feed and grow. After another few years they return to the freshwater sites of their birth, where they spawn and then die. This journey, which may cover 5,000 km (over 3,000 miles), is especially remarkable since each fish locates the very stream in which it was spawned.

Other fish species migrate in the opposite direction. In spring, the freshwater eel lays its eggs in the Sargasso Sea, at a depth of some 500 metres (about 1,700 ft). Translucent leaf-shaped larvae hatch in the summer and are carried by the Gulf Stream to European and North American shores. The journey takes two to three years, during which the eels mature. Five to fifteen years after their arrival in fresh water, they metamorphose into their final marine form and head back to the Sargasso Sea, some 6,000 km (3,700 miles) distant.

The seas' ancient reptilian mariners, the turtles, also use ocean currents as mobile nurseries. Ungainly on land, they are only ashore for a few brief moments as hatchlings, and again, much later, when they return to nest. Little is known about the intervening years, and especially about where the currents carry the juveniles during that time. Young green turtles have been found in the Caribbean among rafts of floating sargassum weed, and probably feed on the small invertebrate animals which also collect in these convergence zones. Other nurseries may exist in the western Mediterranean, where large numbers of juvenile loggerhead turtles have recently been found.

The feeding and nesting sites of many turtle populations are extraordinarily far apart. Loggerheads follow their favoured prey, jellyfish, into northern and sub-Arctic waters; but the same animals breed on the distant shores of Central America. The journey back to their hatching beaches involves prodigious feats of navigation and memory, particularly since turtles may mature at sea for twenty or thirty years before returning home to breed. All in all it is a hazardous lifestyle: nesting females, eggs and hatchlings are particularly vulnerable to predators, and added pressure from humans means that all marine turtle species are now endangered.

Above the ocean surface roam some of the greatest oceanic travellers, the seabirds. The wandering albatross is a supreme exploiter of the winds of the Roaring Forties, the cold seas between 40° and 50° south. With a wingspan of more than 3.5 metres (11.5 ft), the albatross is a superlative glider, built for ocean storms. Albatrosses can travel tens of thousands of kilometres without ever touching land, and may circle the Antarctic continent several times in one year.

In contrast, Wilson's storm-petrel is one of the world's smallest seabirds, at only 15 cm (6 in) long. Nevertheless, it migrates huge distances, nesting in and around Antarctica but flying as far as California and Labrador for the northern summer. The Arctic tern is the greatest traveller of all. It flies half way round the world to catch both polar summers, and sees more daylight each year than any other creature.

At every level above and below the sea, a carnival of animals achieve miraculous journeys. Some are principally passengers, riding moving conveyors of air and water. Others forge through the water to particular geographical goals to feed or breed, guided by sensory capabilities still only guessed at. All, however, live subject to a massive global mechanism of circulating air and water, and to the shifting centres of productivity governed by the oceans' seasonal and circulatory rhythms. Their superbly specialized lifestyles are a product of hundreds of millions of years of biological adaptation; yet in a few brief seconds of evolutionary time, we human beings are changing the atmosphere of our planet, disturbing this mechanism, and threatening their very existence.

67   MASSED FUR SEALS, SOUTH GEORGIA ISLANDS
(Gerry Ellis)
THE SEAL-LIKE MARINE MAMMALS ARE DIVIDED INTO TWO 'SUPERFAMILIES': THE SEA LIONS, FUR SEALS AND WALRUSES FORM THE FIRST, AND THE 'TRUE' SEALS THE SECOND. THOSE IN THE FIRST GROUP ARE ABLE TO TURN THEIR HIND FLIPPERS FORWARD FOR WALKING ON LAND. TRUE SEALS CANNOT DO THIS. SPECIES IN BOTH SUPERFAMILIES DISPERSE OVER THE OCEANS FOR MOST OF THE YEAR, BUT GATHER IN HIGH DENSITIES AT BREEDING TIMES ON BEACHES LIKE THIS, TO RAISE THEIR YOUNG AND MATE.

69

68   CALIFORNIA SEA LIONS

(Richard Herrmann)

SEA LIONS ARE SUPERBLY ADAPTED
TO LIFE IN THE WATER, WITH THEIR
STRONG FLIPPERS AND SLEEK,
STREAMLINED BODIES WELL
COVERED BY A THICK LAYER OF
FAT, WHICH SERVES AS AN ENERGY
STORE AS WELL AS TO INSULATE.
SEA LIONS CAN DIVE RAPIDLY TO A
DEPTH OF UP TO 250 METRES (820
FT), AND MAY STAY SUBMERGED
FOR UP TO EIGHT MINUTES. THEY
INHABIT THE WATERS OF THE
SOUTHERN HEMISPHERE AND·THE
NORTH PACIFIC OCEAN.

70

**69   A SOUTHERN ELEPHANT SEAL,
ANTARCTICA**

(Gerry Ellis)

DURING THE NINETEENTH
CENTURY ELEPHANT SEALS WERE
HUNTED TO NEAR-EXTINCTION FOR
THEIR FUR, BUT THANKS TO
PROTECTIVE MEASURES THEIR
POPULATIONS ARE NOW RISING.

**70   A MOTHER HARP SEAL AND HER
PUP, GULF OF ST LAWRENCE**

(Heather Angel)

HARP SEALS DON'T EVEN VISIT
LAND TO BREED. FOR JUST TWO
WEEKS EARLY IN THE YEAR,
THOUSANDS OF FEMALES GATHER
ON THE 'WHELPING PATCHES' OF
THE ARCTIC ICE TO BEAR THEIR
YOUNG. THEN THE COLONY
MIGRATES TO WARMER WATERS,
WHERE THEY ALL DISPERSE UNTIL
THE NEXT BREEDING SEASON.

71

72

73

71, 72 and 73 CALIFORNIA SEA LIONS (Richard Herrmann), **KILLER WHALES** (Flip Nicklin/
Minden Pictures) **AND BOTTLENOSE DOLPHINS** (Flip Nicklin/Minden Pictures)
LIKE MANY OCEAN MAMMALS, ALL OF THESE TRAVEL IN GROUPS. KILLER WHALES
ARE THE BIGGEST OF THE DOLPHINS, SOMETIMES OVER 9 METRES (30 FT) LONG.
THEY MAY GATHER IN 'PODS' OF 5 TO 100 ANIMALS, AND THEY HUNT IN PACKS;
THEIR DIET VARIES. SOME PODS FEED MOSTLY ON FISH. OTHERS SPECIALIZE IN
CATCHING SEALS, PENGUINS, OTHER DOLPHINS AND THE SMALLER WHALES.
BOTTLENOSE DOLPHINS, SUCH AS THOSE THAT LIVE OFF THE EAST COAST OF THE
USA, OFTEN WINTER IN THE WARMER WATERS OFF FLORIDA. THESE CREATURES
ARE CAPABLE OF A VERY WIDE RANGE OF BEHAVIOUR – FROM THAT OF INSHORE
SOLITARY TO MEMBER OF AN OFFSHORE HERD OF SEVERAL HUNDRED.

74

75

76

74 DIVING HUMPBACKS, STEPHEN'S PASSAGE, ALASKA

(Duncan Murrell/Planet Earth)

FOUND IN BOTH POLAR REGIONS FOR HALF OF THE YEAR, HUMPBACKS FOLLOW
ESTABLISHED MIGRATORY ROUTES BETWEEN THE POLAR SEAS – THEIR FEEDING
GROUNDS DURING THE SUMMER – AND WARMER WATERS, WHERE THEY RAISE
THEIR YOUNG. WHALES' NOSTRILS ARE EQUIPPED WITH VALVES THAT CLOSE
WHEN THEY DIVE. MOST MUST SURFACE EVERY 15 TO 20 MINUTES TO BREATHE,
BUT SOME OF THE TOOTHED WHALES CAN REMAIN SUBMERGED FOR AN HOUR OR
MORE.

75 BREACHING HUMPBACKS

(James D. Watt/Planet Earth)

WHY WHALES BREACH, OR LEAP OUT OF THE WATER, IS NOT FULLY
UNDERSTOOD, BUT HUMPBACKS ARE FREQUENTLY SEEN MAKING SPECTACULAR
LEAPS, SOMETIMES COMPLETELY CLEAR OF THE WATER, THEN CRASHING BACK
INTO THE WAVES.

76 A MINKE WHALE SURFACES THROUGH THE ICE

(Kim Westerskov)

THE MINKE WHALE IS THE SMALLEST OF THE BALEEN WHALES AND IS FOUND
FROM THE POLAR ICE EDGE TO THE TROPICS. AFTER WHALING HAD DEPLETED
THE POPULATIONS OF THE LARGER WHALES – FROM THE 1970S – THIS SPECIES WAS
A SIGNIFICANT TARGET FOR THE WHALING INDUSTRY.

78

77 and 79 SALMON, CANADA (Gilbert van Ryckevorsel/Planet Earth)**, AND LARVAE OF THE COMMON EEL** (Heather Angel)
SOME FISH SPECIES MAKE SPECTACULAR MIGRATIONS BETWEEN FRESH WATER AND THE SEA. SEA SALMON MAY TRAVEL 5,000 KM (OVER 3,000 MILES) TO THEIR HOME STREAMS TO BREED; EELS ARE SPAWNED IN THE SARGASSO SEA BUT THEIR LARVAE MOVE WITH OCEAN CURRENTS FOR THOUSANDS OF KILOMETRES TO THE FRESHWATER SHORES OF EUROPE AND NORTH AMERICA. FIVE TO 15 YEARS LATER, THEY RETURN TO THE SARGASSO TO BREED.

78 A GREEN TURTLE, BORNEO (Linda Pitkin)
THE TURTLE LAYS ITS EGGS, AND BURIES THEM, ON ANCESTRAL HATCHING BEACHES ABOVE THE HIGH-TIDE LINE. THE JUVENILES HATCH ON SHORE, BUT IMMEDIATELY HEAD FOR THE OCEAN. LITTLE IS KNOWN ABOUT WHERE THEY SPEND THEIR FIRST FEW YEARS; IT'S ASSUMED THAT THEY DRIFT WITH THE CURRENT, FEEDING ON SMALL ANIMALS. AFTER TWENTY OR THIRTY YEARS THEY RETURN, BY REMARKABLE FEATS OF NAVIGATION AND MEMORY, TO BREED AT THE SITE OF THEIR OWN HATCHING.

79

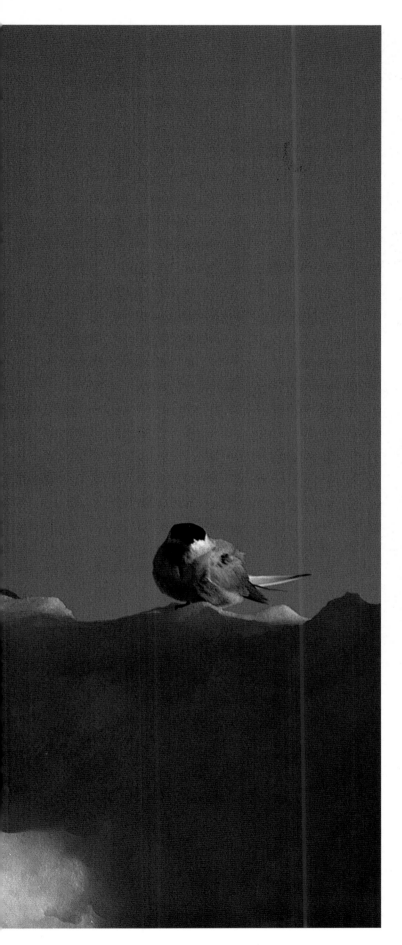

81

82

80, 81 and 82   ARCTIC TERNS (Norbert Rosing), **WHITE-TAILED TROPIC-BIRDS OF
THE SEYCHELLES** (Mike Birkhead/OSF), **AND A SHEARWATER** (Kim Westerskov)
ALL TERNS ARE SKILLED AND GRACEFUL FLIERS – SOME ARE ALSO CALLED
'SEA SWALLOWS'. THE ARCTIC TERN IS THE MOST REMARKABLE AVIAN
VOYAGER OF ALL: IT FLIES POLE TO POLE TO CATCH BOTH POLAR SUMMERS.
TROPIC-BIRDS ARE OCEAN TRAVELLERS SO SPECIALIZED THAT, THOUGH
THEY ARE SUPERB SWIMMERS AND DIVERS, THEY CAN BARELY WALK, OR
EVEN STAND, ON LAND. ALMOST ALWAYS IN THE WATER OR FLYING,
SHEARWATERS GLIDE LOW ALONG WAVE TROUGHS IN SEARCH OF FISH.
THEY COME TO LAND ONLY TO NEST AND RAISE THEIR CHICKS.

CHAPTER FIVE

EAT OR BE EATEN:
GAMBLING FOR SURVIVAL
Dr Martin Angel

Life is a lottery, and to win what they need all creatures have to gamble. This is especially true in the vast and unpredictable ocean environment, where predators are many and food supplies erratic. There are dangers and uncertainties inherent in every activity. But animals have evolved some remarkable strategies which work to minimize these risks.

To be successful, an animal must find enough food to grow to maturity, then search out a mate and successfully launch the next generation – and escape being eaten by others in the process. Given the hazards of life in the seas, the risk of failure is high. Selecting a place in which to feed or spawn presents a particular problem for sea creatures, because the areas richest in food are also the most dangerous in terms of predators. Plant life can thrive only at the upper, sunlit levels of the ocean; this supports populations of tiny herbivores, which in turn attract mini-carnivores and larger predators. In the dark waters beneath the sunlit zone there is less life of all kinds. An animal living there has fewer potential enemies, but pays the price because food is much more difficult to find.

Despite this and other dilemmas, marine animals have evolved some remarkable strategies for successfully feeding and breeding in the seas. But here, as in any environment, there is no such thing as a free lunch: each strategy entails a compromise between cost in energy and the probable danger to an individual or its offspring.

For example, many animals are commuter feeders. They spend the daylight hours deep within the water column where

---

83 A YELLOWHEAD JAWFISH BROODING EGGS, GRAND CAYMAN
(J. Michael Kelly)
THE MALE JAWFISH INCUBATES THE EGGS IN HIS MOUTH FOR FOUR OR FIVE
DAYS. PART OF HIS CARE INVOLVES SPITTING THE EGG MASS OUT INTO THE
CURRENT, IN ORDER TO AERATE THE CONTENTS, AND THEN SUCKING IT BACK IN.

predation is lower, but swim up to the food-rich surface layers at night, when hunters cannot see them. Most of these migrations span just a few hundred metres, but some lanternfish species daily commute over 1,500 metres (nearly a mile) up and down again – a journey which can take three hours each way. In relation to their size, some smaller animals make even more remarkable journeys. Two-millimetre (0.08-in) copepods, the commonest planktonic animals, migrate 500 metres twice a day. Scale up these distances, and the result is comparable with our running a marathon before breakfast and another after supper. Evolution has deemed these huge investments in energy worthwhile because they greatly reduce the risk of predation.

Such animals can 'afford' to make large energetic investments because they have access to plentiful supplies of food. At very deep levels of the ocean, food is extremely scarce – so drastic savings in energy are required. Here, evolution favours giving up organs that are too expensive to run, so brains are small, muscles watery and skeletons weak. Most animals have adopted highly lethargic lifestyles, because any energy spent looking for food is likely to be in vain – and if loss exceeds income, death is the price. So prey is lured. Deep-dwelling fishes often have huge gaping mouths fitted with lethal backward-curving teeth; once seized, a victim rarely escapes. Stomachs are extensible – so much so that the prey may be equal in size to the predator. If you do not eat it, it will eat you!

Eggs and larvae are easy targets for opportunistic predators, so most marine reproductive strategies 'allow for' some losses. From species to species, though, there is still huge variation in the number of offspring, and the energy expended in each one. Sunfish may produce an astonishing ten million eggs, but these have no yolk for the larvae to feed on; all the investment is in numbers. As soon as the larvae hatch they have to start feeding. Tiny and ultra-vulnerable, many will starve and others will be eaten – but from such a vast brood, some will survive.

Krill, on the other hand, which are food for the great whales in the Southern Ocean, invest considerable energy in each of a few hundred offspring. The heavy, yolky eggs sink to great depths where there are far fewer predators, and then hatch. The developing larvae live on their yolk and need no other food as they swim slowly and laboriously to the surface. Once there, they have grown too big for the commoner mini-predators to eat, and are ready to start feeding for themselves. Some of the deep-living brilliant scarlet prawns lay just a few tens of very large-yolked eggs. The parent carries these few precious offspring around on its legs until they hatch, when they are relatively mature and much less vulnerable.

In high-risk coastal environments, animals tend to breed as soon as they can, and carry on producing brood after brood until the 'sharks' get them. In safer, more predictable habitats, animals can afford not to be so profligate. Thus the giant opossum shrimp, which dwells deep beneath the sea's surface, lives a miserly existence using what little food is available to grow very slowly for seven years or more. It then blows all its carefully hoarded investment at once, producing a few tens of eggs before dying.

Different sorts of strategies are adopted by animals when they need to attract a mate. Finding a receptive partner in the ocean's huge, constantly moving volume of water is no easy task. Many animals have found a way round this problem by spawning *en masse*, mysteriously gathering in a particular place at a particular time, apparently prompted by phases of the lunar cycle. Palola worms spawn in this way, but each individual takes the added precaution of splitting in two: one half stays safely in the mud while the other swims to the surface with its fellows. The massed worms provide a feeding bonanza for hordes of fish, but are so numerous that the predators are satiated long before all the worms – and their eggs – are devoured. Indeed, any kind of signal to your own species is also likely to alert predators. Other animals advertise their readiness to mate using pungent scents, gaudy colours, or, in the darkness of the deep sea, flamboyant light displays. Yet the risk of drawing enemies is worth taking; attracting a mate is crucial if the species is to survive.

Sometimes even your own mate must be persuaded that you are not lunch. Male anglerfish are small, active creatures with well developed eyes and large 'noses'. These help them to seek out females, which are quite different animals – sluggish, poorly sighted, and several times bigger. The snack-sized male has to dodge the female's attempts to eat him before fastening himself to her side. There he lives out his life as an external parasite, presumably knowing when he is required to perform by being linked to her hormonal system.

Other unusual sexual practices abound in the sea. Many species are hermaphrodite, and some individuals are even able to fertilize their own eggs. Surprisingly, very few species do without sex entirely, but some animal groups, like the gelatinous salps, do alternate between sexual and asexual reproduction. So successful are they that at times net hauls contain nothing but jelly.

Sex changes are common. Most of the colourful wrasses and parrotfish, for example, begin their lives as similar-looking dull-coloured males or females. Some of the females, however, are able to change sex to become brilliantly patterned males, which then dominate all other males and unchanged females. The changeling males spawn with a long series of chosen female partners; other males may only spawn randomly in large groups, and so have far less chance of passing on their genes.

A less extreme solution to the problems of reproduction is found among some of the tiny ostracods, where the male does all the chasing. Such males are often short-lived, burning themselves out in a frenzied search for willing females. Their chase may well be fruitless, for the females store sperm from just one mating, which they then use to fertilize a long series of broods. In such species, sex ratios are rarely the conventional one to one – perhaps ten females to every one male.

An individual's success may well depend on its ability to vary its behaviour according to circumstance. For example, when food is plentiful, an animal will invest some energy in growth but reserve some for reproduction or as a guarantee against future shortages. When it is scarce, the choices are stark: a hungry animal must migrate to find food, use up its reserves, live a hand-to-mouth existence, or starve. Furthermore, priorities change, and the risks an animal will run to achieve certain goals increase or decrease accordingly. Feeding and avoiding predators are the primary goals for growing larvae, while producing offspring is of paramount importance for mature animals. Many undergo considerable dangers to do so; adult turtles and salmon, for example, travel thousands of exhausting and hazardous kilometres to their home waters simply to breed.

Each reproductive and feeding strategy is a kind of gamble, for none are foolproof: but the odds of risk and reward have been carefully selected by evolution over millions of years. Although the approaches adopted by some animals can seem bizarre to us landlubbers, there is clearly method in what at first sight may look like evolutionary madness.

84 A CLOWN-FISH IN AN ANEMONE, AUSTRALIA

(David Hall)

CLOWN-FISH LIVE IN THE STINGING TENTACLES OF ANEMONES. EACH DERIVES
PROTECTION FROM THE OTHER. THE CLOWN-FISH'S BRILLIANT TERRITORIAL
DISPLAYS, THOUGH AIMED AT ITS OWN MALE RIVALS, ALSO DETER CREATURES
THAT WOULD HARM THE ANEMONE; AND THE ANEMONE'S POWERFUL STING
DETERS THOSE THAT WOULD PREY ON THE CLOWN-FISH.

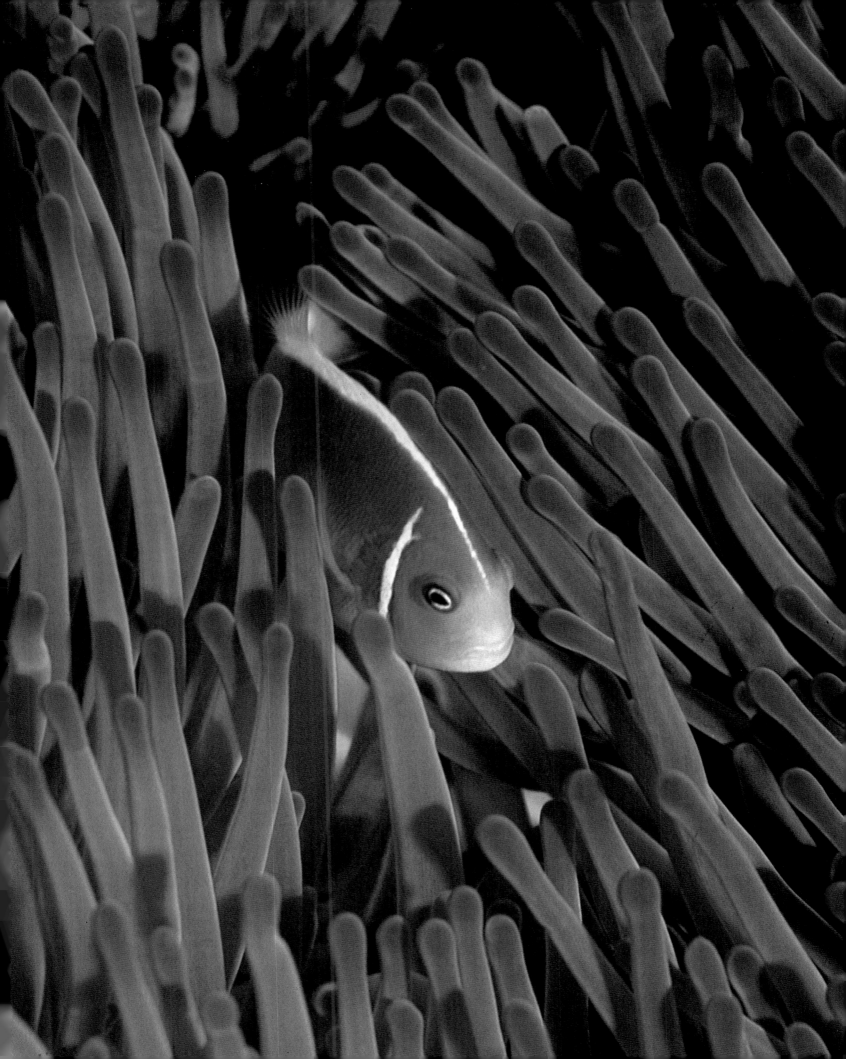

85

85   A HARLEQUIN TUSKFISH, BARRIER REEF, AUSTRALIA

(Norbert Wu)

THIS DAZZLING FISH IS COMMON ALL OVER THE REEF, EATING CRUSTACEANS
AND MOLLUSCS. IT IS A WRASSE, AND AS WITH ALL WRASSE – PARROTFISH,
GROUPERS, ANGELFISH AND OTHERS – SEX CHANGES OCCUR DURING THE LIFE
CYCLE OF SOME INDIVIDUALS: SOME FEMALES BECOME MALES. THESE
CHANGELING MALES ARE DOMINANT OVER OTHER MALES. WHILE THOSE BORN AS
MALES HAVE THE GAUDIEST COLOURING, 'CHANGED' FEMALES ARE SLIGHTLY
LESS ARRESTING, AND FEMALES AND JUVENILES ARE USUALLY DRAB.

86

86 A QUEEN ANGELFISH, CARIBBEAN

(Norbert Wu)

A SINGLE MALE ANGELFISH USUALLY LIVES WITH A HAREM OF FEMALES. WHEN MATING, IT NUZZLES THE FEMALE'S SIDE OR BELLY FOR SEVERAL MINUTES BEFORE THE PAIR SUDDENLY DASH FOR THE SURFACE TO SIMULTANEOUSLY RELEASE SPERM AND THOUSANDS OF EGGS INTO THE WATER.

87

87 A CORAL GROUPER, BARRIER REEF, AUSTRALIA

(Norbert Wu)

AS WITH ALL GROUPERS, SOME FEMALES OF THIS SPECIES LATER BECOME MALES; IN FACT, LARGER AND OLDER CORAL GROUPERS ARE PREDOMINANTLY MALES. SINCE THE SPECIES IS FISHED FOR FOOD AND BIGGER SPECIMENS ARE PREFERRED, POPULATIONS MAY BE LEFT WITHOUT ENOUGH MALES TO SUCCESSFULLY REPRODUCE.

88

88   A SPOTTED CLEANER SHRIMP ON AN ANEMONE, GRAND CAYMAN
(J. Michael Kelly)
THIS SHRIMP, 1-2 CM (.4-1 IN) LONG, IS COMMON THROUGHOUT THE CARIBBEAN,
WHERE IT OFTEN LIVES WITHIN THE TENTACLES OF THE GIANT ANEMONE. IT
FEEDS BY SCOURING THE MOUTHS AND GILLS OF FISH FOR HARMFUL PARASITES.
THE ANEMONE AFFORDS IT PROTECTION FROM PREDATORS, WHILE THE SHRIMP
GAINS EXTRA NOURISHMENT BY FEEDING ON THE SCRAPS THAT THE ANEMONE
LEAVES. BEFORE THEY CAN INHABIT THE ANEMONE, SUCH SHRIMPS 'IMMUNIZE'
THEMSELVES BY PICKING AT THE TENTACLES FOR SEVERAL HOURS.

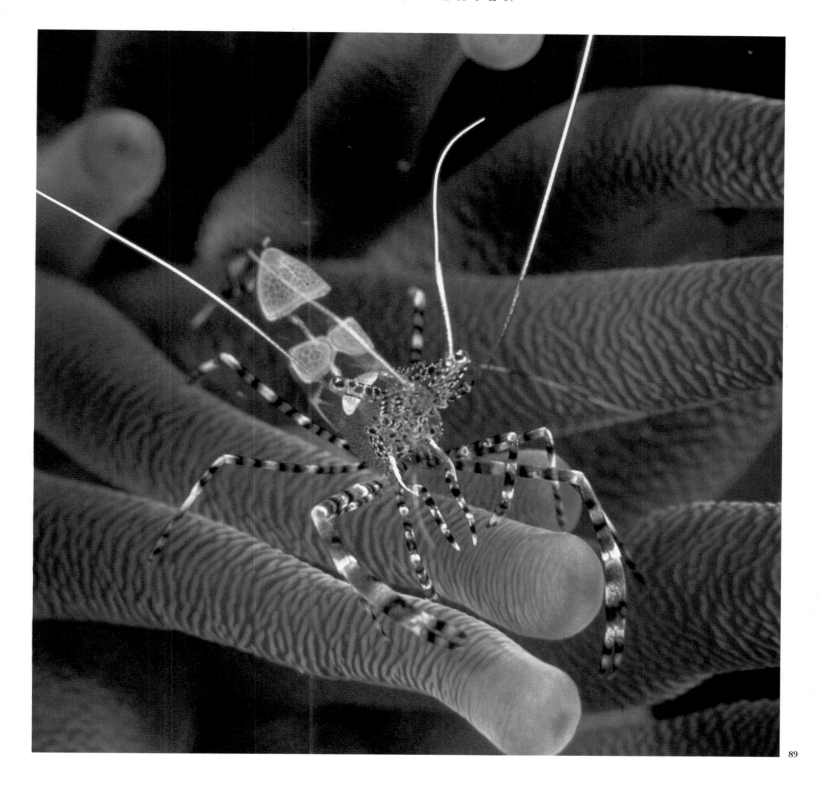

89   *PERICLIMENES YUCATANICUS* ON AN ANEMONE, CARIBBEAN
(B. Jones & M. Shimlock)
THIS CLEANER SHRIMP COHABITS WITH A VARIETY OF ANEMONES, WORKING
OVER THE TENTACLES AND BASE FOR DETRITUS. OCCASIONALLY IT CLEANS FISH
AS WELL, CONSUMING THE PARASITES IN THEIR GILLS AND MOUTHS. PERCHED
ON THE ANEMONE'S TENTACLES, IT WAVES ITS CLAWS IN ORDER TO ATTRACT THE
FISH TO THE 'CLEANING STATION'.

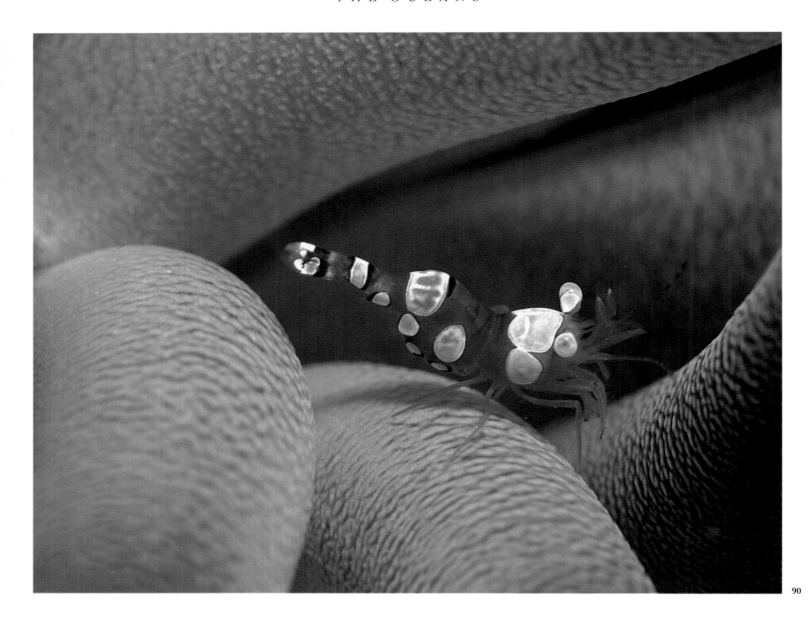

90

90 A SQUAT ANEMONE SHRIMP IN AN ANEMONE, LITTLE CAYMAN

(David Hall)

NOT ONE OF THE CLEANER SHRIMPS, THIS ONE GROWS TO A MAXIMUM 1 CM (.4
IN). IT IS SHY, AND WILL RETREAT INTO THE TENTACLES WHEN APPROACHED.
SOME SHRIMP SPECIES ARE NEVER FOUND SEPARATE FROM ANEMONES – THEIR
RELATIONSHIP WITH THEIR HOST IS OBLIGATE.

91 ANOTHER *PERICLIMENES* ON AN ANEMONE, SIPADAN, MALAYSIA

(B. Jones & M. Shimlock)

THIS TINY SHRIMP, ALSO RATHER SELF-EFFACING, HELPS NOT FISH, BUT ITS
ANEMONE HOST, TO STAY CLEAN. RATHER THAN RESTING ON THE TENTACLES, IT
ENTERS THE ACTUAL MOUTH OF THE ANEMONE TO REACH ITS INNER PARTS.

92

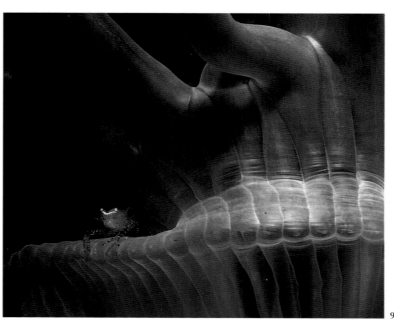

93

92   A HERMIT CRAB ON FIRE CORAL, IN THE RED SEA AT NIGHT
(Jeffrey L. Rotman)
HERMIT CRABS ARE FOUND IN SHALLOW COASTAL WATERS THROUGHOUT THE WORLD, BUT ESPECIALLY AMONG CORAL REEFS. RATHER THAN MANUFACTURING ITS OWN SHELL, THE SOFT-BODIED HERMIT FINDS AND WEARS ONE THAT ANOTHER CREATURE HAS DISCARDED; WHEN IT HAS OUTGROWN IT, THE HERMIT EXCHANGES IT FOR ANOTHER. HERMITS OFTEN SHARE THEIR SHELLS WITH OPOSSUM SHRIMPS AND THEIR YOUNG – THE GUESTS MAY HELP TO KEEP THE SHELL CLEAN.

93   A CLEANER SHRIMP ON THE BASAL DISC OF AN ANEMONE, RED SEA
(Jeffrey L. Rotman)
A SHRIMP'S EXOSKELETON DOES NOT PROVIDE PROTECTION AGAINST THE ANEMONE'S STING. LIKE CLOWN-FISH, WHICH ALSO LIVE AMONGST ANEMONES, THE SHRIMP APPEARS TO ACCLIMATIZE ITSELF TO THE STING, AND LIVES UNHARMED WITHIN ITS HOST.

94

94   A CHAMBERED NAUTILUS, VANUATU, SOUTH PACIFIC OCEAN
(David Hall)
THE NAUTILUS IS ONE OF THE MOST PRIMITIVE CREATURES IN THE SEAS TODAY,
A SURVIVOR OF SOME 500 MILLION YEARS, AND FOUND THROUGHOUT THE INDO-
PACIFIC OCEANS. IT INHABITS DEEP WATERS (UP TO 700 METRES, 2,300 FT) DURING
THE DAY, BUT MIGRATES TO FEED IN SHALLOWER WATERS (30-60 METRES, 100-200
FT) BY NIGHT. IT CONTROLS ITS BUOYANCY – ITS ASCENT AND DESCENT – BY
REGULATING THE PROPORTIONS OF GAS AND WATER IN THE CHAMBERS OF ITS
SPECIALIZED SHELL.

95

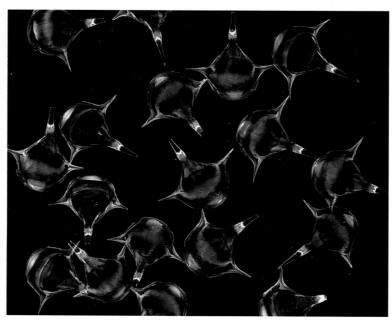

96

95   OSTRACODS (*VARGULA CYPRIDINA*)

(P.J. Herring/IOS)
THESE 2-2.5 MM (ABOUT 0.1 IN)
LONG, DETRITUS-CONSUMING
CREATURES INHABIT CORAL REEFS
IN THE INDO-PACIFIC AREA.
DURING THE DAY THEY HIDE AWAY
AMONGST THE CORAL AND IN THE
SEDIMENT. THEN AT NIGHT THEY
SWIM TO THE SURFACE, SETTING
THE OCEAN ALIGHT WITH THEIR
EERIE BLUE LUMINESCENCE,
WHICH THEY RELEASE INTO THE
WATER FROM GLANDS ON THEIR
UPPER LIPS.

96   PTEROPODS, *DIACRIA MAJOR*, NORTH EAST ATLANTIC

(Heather Angel)
THESE TINY 'WINGED' MOLLUSCS
GENERALLY FUNCTION FIRST AS
MALES AND THEN AS FEMALES,
LAYING GELATINOUS MASSES OF
STICKY EGGS. BUT WHEN FOOD IS
SCARCE AND ENERGY CANNOT BE
EXPENDED ON SEXUAL
REPRODUCTION, THEY BECOME
HERMAPHRODITES, SHEDDING
THEIR SHELLS, SHRINKING IN SIZE
AND SPLITTING INTO SEVERAL
ANIMALS.

97

97 A SQUID, *LOLIGO OPALESCENS*,
AND ITS EGGS, CALIFORNIA
(Richard Herrmann)
NAMED *OPALESCENS* FOR ITS
IRIDESCENT EYES, THIS SQUID
SPAWNS IN VAST NUMBERS IN
MONTEREY BAY, SOUTH OF SAN
FRANCISCO. IT SPAWNS JUST ONCE
IN ITS LIFETIME, AND THEN DIES.
INVESTING HARD-WON ENERGY IN
A SINGLE BURST OF
REPRODUCTION IS A COMMON
STRATEGY AMONG MARINE
ANIMALS.

98 OCTOPUS EGGS HATCHING
(Norbert Wu)
LIKE SQUID (97), OCTOPUSES SPAWN
JUST ONCE BEFORE DYING. THE
YOUNG LOOK JUST LIKE ADULTS,
BUT MEASURE A MERE 3 CM (1 IN
APPROX.) INCLUDING THEIR
TENTACLES. OCTOPUSES SPAWN *EN
MASSE*, BUT DIVIDE THE AVAILABLE
SEA-FLOOR SPACE INTO
TERRITORIES – CLUSTERS OF EGGS
ARE SEEN AT REGULAR INTERVALS.
TERRITORY IS ALL-IMPORTANT FOR
THE HATCHING YOUNG, WHICH
GROW RAPIDLY. THE BEST SPOTS,
PROVIDING PLENTY OF FOOD, ARE
AT THE CENTRE OF THE MASS; AT
THE OUTSKIRTS, THE OFFSPRING
ARE VULNERABLE TO PREDATORS
AND MAY FIND FOOD HARD TO
COME BY.

98

99

99   A BLACK SWALLOWER, WITH PREY

(Norbert Wu)

IN THE DEEP SEA WHERE THIS FISH LIVES, FOOD IS SCARCE AND ANY
OPPORTUNITY MUST BE SEIZED. MANY ANIMALS ARE CAPABLE OF EATING PREY AS
LARGE AS THEMSELVES – A CASE OF 'EAT, OR BE EATEN'. SUCH CREATURES MAY
FEED ONLY ONCE EVERY FEW MONTHS; THEIR STOMACHS TAKE TIME TO DIGEST
THE FOOD, WHICH PROVIDES A SLOW-RELEASE ENERGY STORE.

100   DEEP-SEA ANGLERFISH, *LINOPHRYNE INDICA*: A FEMALE AND A DWARF MALE

(Norbert Wu)

MANY TIMES BIGGER THAN THE MALE ANGLERFISH, BUT SLUGGISH AND POORLY
SIGHTED, THE FEMALE ATTEMPTS TO DEVOUR HIM WHEN HE APPROACHES HER.
BUT, WITH HIS AGILITY AND SUPERIOR VISION, HE USUALLY MANAGES TO FASTEN
HIMSELF TO HER SIDE WITH HIS LITTLE JAWS BEFORE SHE HAS A CHANCE TO
GOBBLE HIM UP. HIS MOUTH SOON FUSES WITH HER SKIN AND EVENTUALLY
THEIR CIRCULATORY SYSTEMS MERGE. NOW ESSENTIALLY A SACK OF SPERM, THE
MALE RECEIVES ALL HIS NUTRIENTS VIA HIS HOSTESS. IN THE EMPTY DEPTHS OF
THE OCEAN, THIS STRATEGY ENSURES THAT THEY WILL BE TOGETHER WHEN THE
FEMALE IS READY TO BREED.

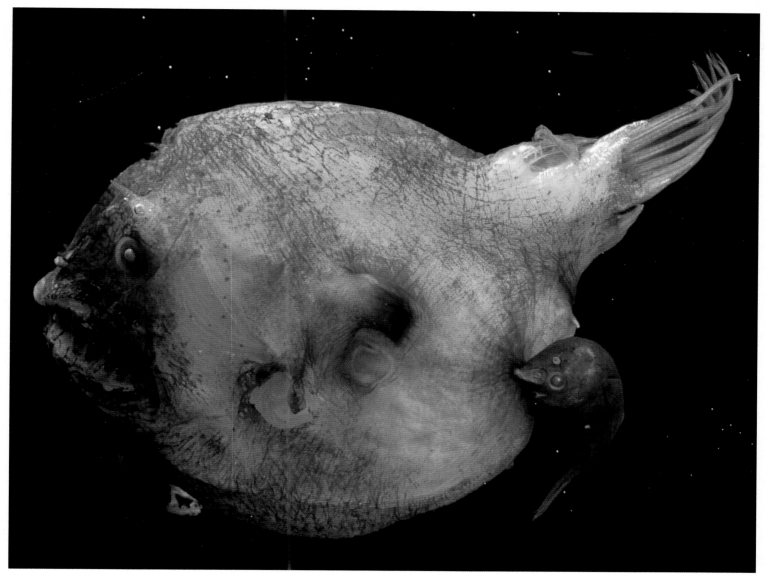

100

101   **A DEEP-SEA ANGLERFISH
LARVA, CELEBES SEA, INDONESIA**
(Norbert Wu)
ANGLERFISH BEGIN THEIR LIVES AS
LARVAE DWELLING CLOSE TO THE
SEA'S SURFACE, WHERE FOOD IS
PLENTIFUL. THE BUBBLE-LIKE
STRUCTURE AROUND THE LARVA
(SHOWN HERE) IS A BUOYANCY
DEVICE. AS IT BEGINS TO
METAMORPHOSE INTO THE ADULT
FORM, IT WILL MIGRATE TO THE
DEPTHS, WHERE IT WILL SPEND
THE REST OF ITS LIFE.

101

CHAPTER SIX

DANCING IN THE DARK:
SIGNALLING IN A SUNLESS WORLD
Dr Peter Herring

*Signalling or seeing, hiding or hunting, luring or decoying —
colour and pattern are basic to communication and concealment
among animals in the ocean, as in the rest of the natural
world. At shallow, sunlit levels, flamboyant colour signals
resemble those of land animals. But in the gloomy abyss
beneath, colour has little function: here, creatures communicate
with light.*

W E HUMANS TEND TO SEE COLOUR IN TERMS OF THE
pleasure it gives us, but nature has more practical con-
cerns. Many animals living in the well lit waters of the ocean
shallows have colour vision and use colours in a number of dazzling ways. The brilliant display of the Pacific Ocean clown-
fish, for instance, attracts predators, which themselves become
prey when they pursue the clown-fish down into the stinging
tentacles of the anemones amongst which it lives. The flying
gurnard, inhabitant of the warmer waters of the Atlantic and
the Red Sea, when threatened spreads its massive pectoral fins
in a startling display of blue designed to make it appear larger
than life.

Pattern and form may help an animal to merge with its surroundings or to stand out from them; to attract a mate, or prey,
or to frighten off a predator. Many marine animals can change
their colour or patterning at will, and are masters of camouflage: plaice and other flatfish can merge almost completely,
within minutes, with the gravel, sand or mud on which they are
lying. Others, like the spotted scorpion-fish, found in all the
oceans, lies motionless and undetectable against the seabed,
waiting to pounce on passing crustaceans and other prey.

---

102 A SCHOOL OF TARPON, GRAND CAYMAN
(J. Michael Kelly)
AT MID-OCEAN DEPTHS ONLY A LITTLE LIGHT IS AVAILABLE. RED AND YELLOW
ARE FILTERED OUT, LEAVING JUST THE SHORTER BLUE-GREEN WAVELENGTHS
VISIBLE. MOST FISH LIVING AT THESE LEVELS HAVE EVOLVED EYES THAT ARE
SENSITIVE ONLY TO BLUE-GREEN PIGMENTS.

But in the open ocean there is no background against which to be seen, except – and this only at the surface – for the ripple and shimmer of the water itself. Then, as you descend, the scatter of light above you rapidly dims and colours begin to change. Long red and yellow wavelengths are soon filtered out – only 25 metres (about 80 ft) down, a red object looks black. Shorter wavelengths penetrate furthest, and deeper down a blue-green light prevails, its intensity diminishing tenfold with every 70 metres' (230 ft) depth – providing a daytime moonlight at 450 metres (nearly 1,500 ft), starlight at 600 (nearly 2,000 ft), total blackness at 900.

Yet, even as far down as 11,000 metres (nearly 7 miles), animals live. In the absence of ambient light, they have solved the problem by producing their own bioluminescence, and many of them have highly efficient eyes. Numerous kinds of fish, jellyfish, worms, clams, snails, squid, sea-squirts, starfish, shrimps and other crustaceans are able to convert chemical energy into light energy. This is a much more efficient process than that used to create artificial light: whereas only 10 per cent of the power in a lightbulb results in light – the rest is lost in heat – almost 100 per cent of bioluminescent energy is light.

The most stunning luminescence, reported by mariners and explorers for centuries, is that sometimes observed on the ocean at night. On one of his voyages Darwin noted: 'The sea presented a wonderful and most beautiful spectacle . . . the surface glowed with a pale light. [The *Beagle*] drove before her two billows of liquid phosphorus, and in her wake was followed by a milky train.'

Tiny single-called organisms called dinoflagellates, half-plant half-animal, were probably responsible for this spectacular display. Their defensive flashes, produced when some mechanical intruder disturbs them, startle the myriad crustaceans that graze on them, thus interrupting their feeding. As an added bonus, the flashes act as a burglar alarm, alerting larger predators to the crustaceans' presence.

In the Caribbean, waves of light are occasionally seen at night sweeping across sandy reefs. These are the complex luminescent dialogues between male and female crustaceans nicknamed 'firefleas'. Swimming often in synchronously pulsing groups, the males secrete tiny points of light; the females recognize their mates by the pulses' patterns – their frequency, paths and timing – then join the game of follow-my-leader, finally to mate in the dark.

Other bioluminescent phenomena are less easily explained. Much larger waves of light are occasionally seen on the surface of the Indian Ocean, some as fleeting parallel bands, some as vast spinning phosphorescent wheels. The spokes can be hundreds of metres long, and move at over 80 km (50 miles) an hour – faster than any organism. Is this grand light show caused by an underwater earthquake? No one yet has the answer.

Many jellyfish and their relatives the sea-pens produce defensive flashes and glows on contact with other animals. One deep-sea jellyfish looks like a Catherine wheel, with waves of light racing round its body, while others leave a luminous ink behind them as they swim out of the path of danger. There are deep-sea shrimps that squirt bright-blue clouds into the black water, while the brittle-star distracts its enemy in a more elaborate way. If the lights flashing up and down its arms fail to deter, it may shed an armtip – which continues to flash, while the brittle-star, all other lights extinguished, creeps away to safety, leaving its predator with a mere snack instead of a dinner.

An animal that can match its own brightness to that of its background stands a fair chance of survival. Transparency is an excellent means of camouflage, for the gelatinous jellyfish or for the Indian glass-fish and the larvae of soles and plaice. But animals with complex tissues, such as most squid and fish, cannot make themselves transparent. Instead, they may resort to feigning transparency by making their flanks reflective; in the special light conditions prevailing in the sea, a vertical mirror is invisible.

But this mirror camouflage will not fool the waiting, watching predator that sees the fish from below. It will recognize its potential victim as a dark silhouette against the day- or moon-light entering the water from overhead. The solution, for the vulnerable party, is to illuminate the silhouette. Thus, many of the species that inhabit the upper 800 metres (2,600 ft) or so equip their underbellies with rows of lights. Squid, fish and shrimps can even vary the intensity to match that of the light filtering down from above. The hatchet-fish, for instance, perfectly matches the angular distribution of its luminescence and its blueness with the downwelling daylight. A similar camouflage system was successfully tested on torpedo bombers during the Second World War, allowing them to close in on surfaced submarines without being seen against the sky.

Camouflage in the ocean deeps depends on being able to merge imperceptibly into the blackness. Since animals may flash their lights – usually blue – from any angle, uniform colour and a non-reflective matt surface are prerequisites for safety. Velvet black is common among fish, while jellyfish and squid may be dark brown or purple. Strangely (to our terrestrial way of thinking), shrimps are a brilliant scarlet. But since, unlike their shallow-water counterparts, deep-sea animals have no colour vision and only blue light by which to see – many make the most of what light there is by tuning their eyes to blue only – and since blue light is perfectly absorbed by the red pigment, the shrimps are as invisible as any of their black-clad neighbours.

Being able to detect animals in the water column above them is so essential that many fish and crustaceans have evolved eyes designed exclusively for looking upwards. These eyes may be tubular, with a large lens ideal for capturing light from over-head, at the expense of being able to see nothing to the side or below. Eyes that need to detect even the faintest glow in the abyss must be supremely sensitive. Hence the evolution of a reflective layer, familiar to us in the eyes of cats, owls and moths.

In the deep ocean, light can also serve to lure prey. Several families of fish dangle luminous tassels from the lower jaw, perhaps mimicking different kinds of plankton. Many anglerfish offer a tempting luminous 'bait' hanging from the dorsal fin-ray, that they have modified as a fishing-rod. One species can gradually draw back the 'rod', playing in the prey until it is within reach of its immense jaws. These fish provide no light of their own, but make use of the dense cultures of glowing bacteria that inhabit their lures.

The flashlight fish also depends on bacteria for its illumination. The bacterial colonies in the 'headlights' beneath its eyes search out the planktonic prey; in order to turn the headlights off, the host has evolved an eyelid-like shutter. The bacteria harboured by anglerfish and flashlight fish cannot yet be grown in any other medium. How the right bacteria get into the next generation is an unsolved mystery.

As the firefleas' behaviour demonstrates, the language of light is also the language of courtship and mating. Correct recognition is essential: fish, crustaceans and squid all manifest their sexual differences in the sizes or patterns of their lights. 'Conversations' between members of the same species are, of course, hazardous to the participants: many an illuminated exchange must signal the presence of a tasty mouthful to a patrolling predator.

But a very few fish have developed both a headlight which emits deep-red light and a second visual pigment sensitive to it – in effect, a private channel of communication. In addition, this personal sniperscope enables its possessor to observe potential prey without their realizing that they are under surveillance; unlike most other inhabitants of the deep, it will be able to see, for instance, the unwary scarlet shrimp, oblivious to the fatal beam focused on it.

The complexity of such natural equipment and strategies, and the mysterious – almost magical – nature of bioluminescent phenomena, remind us that the oceans still hold many secrets. What we do know is that anything an animal can do with light and colour in the sunlit waters of the tropical reef, another can match in the abyss with light of its own making.

---

103 BIG-EYE TREVALLIES, BORNEO

(Linda Pitkin)

OCEAN FISH ARE COMMONLY SILVERY AND REFLECTIVE. THIS IS A WONDERFULLY EFFECTIVE CAMOUFLAGE DEVICE: JUST AS A VERTICAL MIRROR IS INVISIBLE IN THE SEA'S SPECIAL LIGHT CONDITIONS, SO ARE FISH WITH MIRROR-LIKE SURFACES.

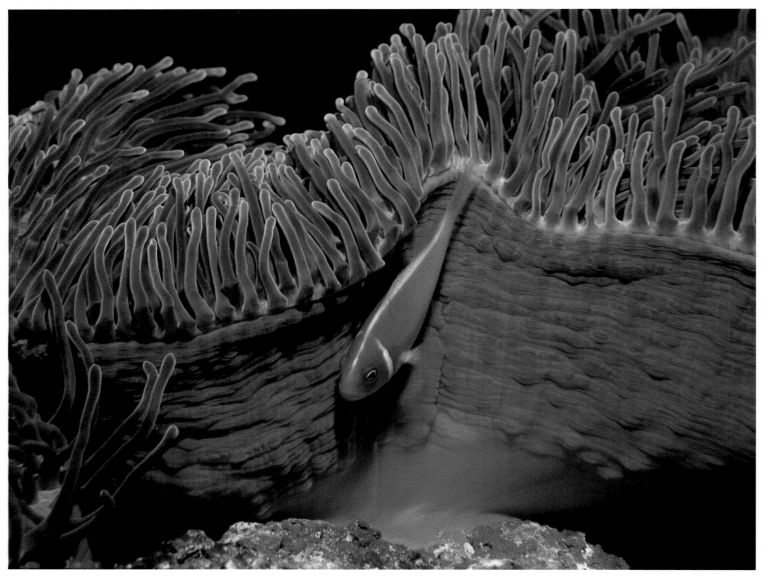

104

105

106

104   A CLOWN-FISH ON AN ANEMONE, SOLOMON ISLANDS

(David Hall)

THERE ARE 26 SPECIES OF CLOWN-FISH, INHABITING 10 SPECIES OF ANEMONE.
THESE VERY COLOURFUL FISH, WHICH LIVE ON CORAL REEFS, ARE
HERMAPHRODITIC – ALL ARE BORN AS MALES, BUT SOME LATER CHANGE INTO
FEMALES. THE FEMALES, WHICH ARE LARGER, ARE THE BOSSES.

105   A BALLED ANEMONE, SOLOMON ISLANDS

(B. Jones & M. Shimlock)

WHY ANEMONES 'BALL UP', OR RETRACT, IS NOT CERTAIN. USUALLY IF ONE IS IN
THAT STATE, SO ARE ITS NEAR NEIGHBOURS. BALLING UP MAY BE A REACTION TO
LOW TIDES OR LOW LIGHT, OR A WAY OF PROTECTING THE MOUTH DISC;
ALTERNATIVELY, THE ANEMONE MAY RETRACT IN ORDER TO UNCOVER THE
CORAL AROUND THE BASE WHEN ITS SYMBIOTIC FISH BEGIN TO SPAWN AND LAY
THEIR EGGS THERE.

106   A CLOWN-FISH, *AMPHIPRION FRENATUS*, IN AN ANEMONE, PHILIPPINES

(David Hall)

CLOWN-FISH APPEAR GRADUALLY TO BUILD UP AN IMMUNITY TO THE ANEMONES'
STING, BY MAKING REPEATED SHORT CONTACT, USUALLY STARTING WITH THE
TAIL. ALSO, THEIR COATING OF SLIME MAY PROTECT THEM.

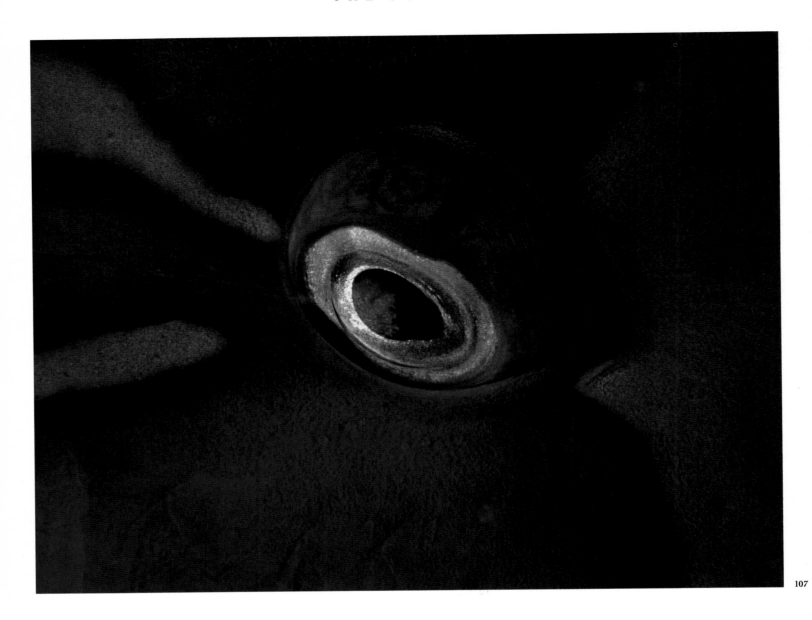

107

107, 108 and 109 PARROTFISH EYES (B. Jones & M. Shimlock)
AND A PUFFERFISH EYE (B. Jones & M. Shimlock)
THE EYES OF MANY CORAL REEF FISH LIKE THESE ARE EXTREMELY SENSITIVE TO
COLOUR, WHICH MAY BE USED TO ATTRACT, WARN OR ADVERTISE. THIS IS IN
MARKED CONTRAST TO THE EYES OF FISH LIVING DEEPER DOWN IN THE OCEAN,
WHERE LIGHT IS LOW: THERE, MOST FISH HAVE NO COLOUR VISION, AND THEIR
EYES ARE TUNED TO BLUE ONLY.

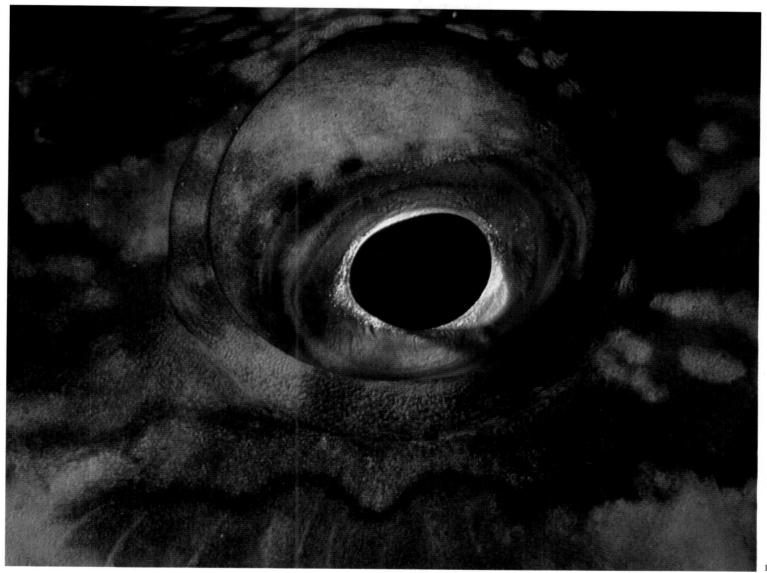

108

109

110

111

112

120

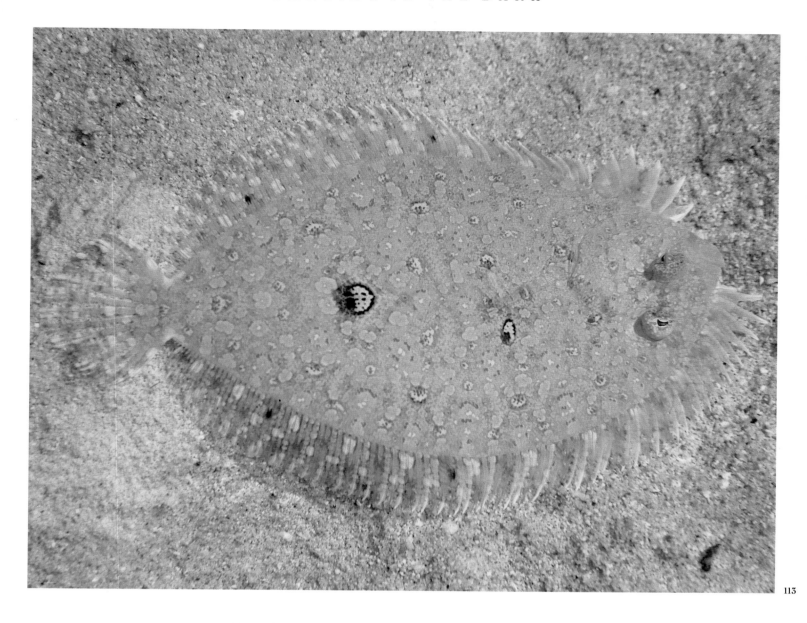

113

110, 111 and 112   A CROCODILE-FISH (Norbert Wu), **AND TWO SCORPION-FISH**
(B. Jones & M. Shimlock)
THE 'HAIRY' GROWTHS AND MOTTLED COLOURING OF THESE REEF INHABITANTS
BLEND ALMOST PERFECTLY WITH THEIR CORAL BACKGROUND. SCORPION-FISH,
UNLIKE CROCODILE-FISH **(110)**, ARE HIGHLY POISONOUS AND CAN GIVE A PAINFUL,
EVEN FATAL, STING IF INADVERTENTLY TRODDEN ON. THEY ARE MAINLY
NOCTURNAL. BY DAY THEIR SUPERB CAMOUFLAGE CONCEALS THEM FROM
PREDATORS AND FROM PREY; BY NIGHT THEY WAIT TO POUNCE ON INCAUTIOUS
VICTIMS.

113   A PEACOCK FLOUNDER, GRAND CAYMAN
(J. Michael Kelly)
MOST FLATFISH LIKE THIS FLOUNDER CAN MERGE INDISTINGUISHABLY WITH THE
SAND OR MUD OF THE SEABED WHERE MOST OF THEM LIVE. MANY ADULTS
ADAPT THE COLOUR OF THEIR PIGMENTED UPPER SIDE TO MATCH THAT OF THE
SEA FLOOR. IDEALLY HIDDEN IN THIS WAY, THESE CARNIVORES LIE IN WAIT FOR
SMALL CRUSTACEANS AND OTHER PREY, WHICH THEY LOCATE WITH THEIR KEEN
SENSE OF SMELL.

114

114   AN ATLANTIC COMB-JELLY AND A JELLYFISH
(Peter Parks/Norbert Wu Photography)
COMB-JELLIES ARE GELATINOUS PLANKTONIC ORGANISMS, NUMBERING ABOUT 90
SPECIES WIDELY DISTRIBUTED IN THE WORLD'S OCEANS. THEY FEED ON SMALLER
PLANKTON AND ARE THEMSELVES PREYED ON BY FISH. THEIR BODIES ARE LITTLE
MORE THAN A THIN CASE AROUND A CAVITY. BUT THE CAVITY IS IN FACT A HUGE
PLANKTON TRAP: ON ENCOUNTERING THEIR PREY, THEY 'VACUUM' IT UP. ONE
SPECIES, FOUND IN THE WEST ATLANTIC, IS THOUGHT TO SWALLOW NEARLY 500
COPEPODS EVERY HOUR. COMB-JELLIES HAVE NO TENTACLES, AND SWIM MOUTH
FIRST. TWO ROWS OF HAIR-LIKE CILIA BEAT SYNCHRONOUSLY TO PROPEL THEM
ALONG. MANY COMB-JELLIES AND JELLYFISH, LIKE THOSE SHOWN HERE, ARE
LUMINESCENT. THE JELLYFISH IS ABOUT THE SIZE OF A FIST AND IS OF AN
EXCEPTIONALLY BRIGHT-SHINING KIND. JELLYFISH RANGE FROM THE OCEAN
SURFACE TO ALMOST ANY DEPTH, AND FROM TROPICAL WATERS TO SUBPOLAR.

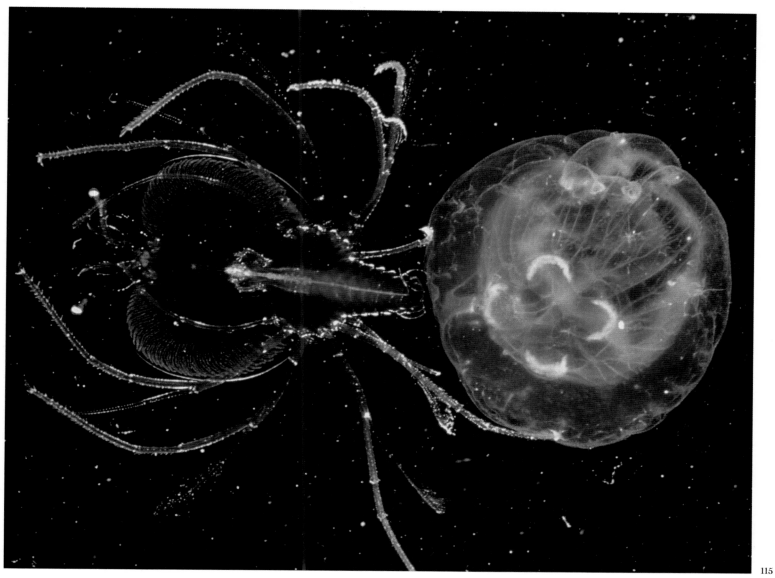

115

115   A LOBSTER LARVA HITCHING A LIFT WITH A MOON JELLY

(Peter Parks/Norbert Wu Photography)

AT LARVAL STAGE, THE WEAK-SWIMMING, TRANSPARENT LOBSTER BEARS LITTLE
RELATION TO ITS ADULT FORM. BEFORE THEY SETTLE ON THE SEABED AND
BEGIN TO LOOK LIKE LOBSTERS AS WE KNOW THEM, THE LARVAE SWIM ABOUT IN
THE PLANKTON FOR A YEAR OR MORE, MOULTING BETWEEN 14 AND 17 TIMES. BUT
BEFORE THEY ARE READY TO SEARCH FOR A SUITABLE PLACE ON THE SEA FLOOR
TO METAMORPHOSE, A HUGE NUMBER OF LARVAE ARE LOST. FOR, APART FROM
THEIR TRANSPARENCY, THEY ARE COMPLETELY UNPROTECTED AGAINST A WIDE
VARIETY OF ENEMIES, FROM WHICH THEY HAVE LITTLE CHANCE OF ESCAPE.
ABOUT 10 PER CENT OF A LARVAL OYSTER SWARM, FOR INSTANCE, IS EATEN EACH
DAY. IN ADDITION, THE LARVAE PREY ON EACH OTHER. CRAB LARVAE FEED ON
LARVAL MOLLUSCS, AND ARE THEMSELVES DEVOURED BY LOBSTER LARVAE.
SOMETIMES LARVAE HITCH A LIFT WITH OTHER ORGANISMS, GAINING EFFORT-
FREE TRANSPORT THROUGH THE SEAS.

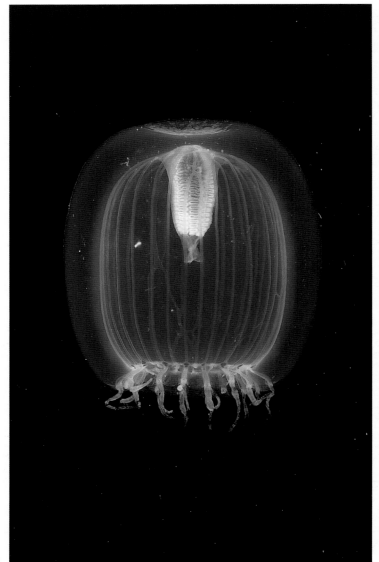

116

1

118

119

116, 117 and 118   LUMINOUS JELLYFISH
(IOS; Norbert Wu; Jeffrey L. Rotman)
MANY JELLYFISH HAVE COLOURED INTERNAL STRUCTURES VISIBLE THROUGH A
TRANSPARENT OR DELICATELY TINTED BELL. SOME PRODUCE GLOWS OR FLASHES
WHEN THEY ARE TOUCHED BY ANOTHER ANIMAL – PROBABLY AS A DEFENCE
MECHANISM INTENDED TO ALARM OR WARN PREDATORS. INTERESTINGLY,
JELLYFISH CANNOT SEE THEIR OWN DISPLAYS, SO THESE REACTIONS HAVE
EVOLVED IN RESPONSE TO OTHERS' EYES.

119   AN ANGLERFISH
(IOS)
THE *MELANOCETUS* ANGLERFISH IS A DEEP-LIVING SPECIES THAT HAS EVOLVED A
SPECIALLY MODIFIED DORSAL FIN – A 'FISHING ROD', WITH ITS LUMINOUS LIGHT
ORGAN AT THE END, ACTING AS 'BAIT'; IN THIS WAY, IT 'CATCHES' SMALL FISH,
SQUID AND CRUSTACEANS. ONCE THE FEROCIOUS TEETH HAVE CLAMPED DOWN
ON THEIR VICTIMS, ONLY THE TINIEST STAND A CHANCE OF SLIPPING BACK INTO
THE WATER.

120   A DEEP-SEA HATCHET-FISH

(Norbert Wu/OSF)

121   A DEEP-LIVING DECAPOD: *EPHYRINA FIGUERIAE*

(Heather Angel)

THIS CREATURE LIVES AT A DEPTH OF ABOUT 1,000 METRES (3,300 FT). BELOW
ABOUT 600 METRES (1,970 FT), MOST ORGANISMS ARE EITHER RED OR BLACK. SINCE
RED IS INVISIBLE AT THESE DEPTHS, IT SERVES AS A CAMOUFLAGE. THE RED
COLOUR RESULTS FROM ACCUMULATED CAROTENOID PIGMENTS, ORIGINALLY
DERIVED FROM PLANT PLANKTON. MOST DEEP-SEA DECAPODS, INCLUDING THIS
SPECIES, EMIT DISGUISING CLOUDS OF LUMINESCENT FLUID WHEN A PREDATOR
DISTURBS THEM.

122   A FLASHLIGHT FISH, INDIAN OCEAN

(Norbert Wu)

THIS DEEP-SEA FISH HAS A LARGE 'HEADLIGHT' BENEATH ITS EYE. THE LIGHT
SOURCE IS NOT ELECTRICAL, BUT DERIVES FROM LUMINESCENT BACTERIA
INHABITING THE LIGHT ORGAN, WHICH THE FISH USES FOR THE PURPOSE OF
ILLUMINATING PREY.

121

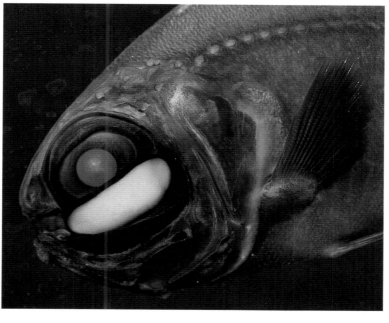

122

CHAPTER SEVEN

FROM ATMOSPHERE TO ABYSS:
THE ENDLESS CYCLE OF ELEMENTS
Dr Andrew Watson

Western culture leaves us ill equipped to contemplate the staggering age of the earth and its oceans. According to the Bible, the earth was made a few hundred generations ago, over one hectic week. The eastern religions, which envisage time as immense and unending, seem to be nearer the truth. In Hindu chronology a kalpa, *one cycle of time within the universal existence, is about 4,300 million years – roughly the age of this planet as we now understand it.*

MORE THAN 3,000 MILLION YEARS AGO, THE FIRST microbes appeared on earth. They developed an intimate relationship with the physics and chemistry of rock, sea and atmosphere, evolving systems to maintain and repair the global environment – eventually providing the right conditions for multi-celled animals to evolve, a mere 900 million years ago. The microbes retain their key role, helping to cycle elements between land and sea, earth and atmosphere. Practically every one of the ninety-odd elements circulates in this way, and those that are most important to life – carbon, nitrogen, oxygen, phosphorus and sulphur – are transferred the most rapidly, since living organisms extract these from their surroundings in order to feed and grow. Other elements are moved around more slowly, by the geological processes that mould the landscape both above and below the oceans. These great cycles serve to correct any imbalances that occur, keeping conditions in any one place more or less constant; without such feedback mechanisms, life as we know it would not survive.

If we imagine the earth as an organism, a single cell perhaps, then the seas are its protoplasm – the liquid in which most of the vital reactions take place. This is more than a trite analogy:

123 **TUBE SPONGES, BELIZE**
(David Hall)
ORGANIC PARTICLES, THE DECOMPOSING FRAGMENTS OF LIVING THINGS, FALL IN A CONSTANT SHOWER THROUGH THE SEA, NOURISHING SCAVENGERS AND ALL KINDS OF FILTER-FEEDERS SUCH AS THESE TUBE SPONGES.

many elements in sea-water occur at strikingly similar concentrations in the cells of living creatures. Those elements which provide the basic building-blocks of life are plentiful in the seas, while toxic ones – heavy metals, for example – are present only in low concentrations. This is no coincidence: life itself is basically a phenomenon of aqueous chemistry, and many of its properties evolved in the oceans and other wet places of the young earth. Evolution used the substances present in these watery environments as its raw materials, and our own bodies bear the legacy to this day.

Other than water, the sea is of course salt – about 3.5 per cent minerals by weight. Ocean salt is not pure sodium chloride, like table salt, but a rich brew which also includes magnesium, sulphate, potassium and calcium, plus traces of most other natural elements. Some of these occur in amounts which, though representing relatively low concentrations, are surprising: a cubic km (roughly a quarter of a cubic mile) of ocean, for instance, contains 50 kg (110 lb) of gold, and some 27 kg (60 lb) of uranium-235 – enough to make several atomic bombs. Perhaps fortunately, no one has yet devised a commercially viable way of extracting them.

Such minerals arrive in the sea by various routes. Most are the products of land erosion, and are borne to the oceans by rivers and glaciers, or as dust blown through the atmosphere. Others enter from the earth's molten interior in volcanic explosions, or through deep fissures in the seabed known as hydrothermal vents – pathways discovered only recently (some as deep as 2.4 km, 1.5 miles). Different substances remain in sea-water for enormously variable time spans; chloride ion, for example, endures for an average of 400 million years, lead only fifty years. Generally, it is the elements which form the most soluble compounds that are most abundant in sea-water. Less soluble compounds tend to disappear relatively quickly because they stick to the solid particles which fall in a constant drizzle through the ocean. At the seabed many kilometres below, such compounds are rapidly buried, then eventually absorbed into the earth's interior.

These drifting, falling particles thus play a vital role in maintaining the composition of sea-water. Most are the remains of phytoplankton, the microscopic plants which grow in the sunlit surface layer of the sea and form the base of the marine food chain. Every litre of surface water contains tens or even hundreds of thousands of their cells, many less than a thousandth of a millimetre (0.00004 in) in diameter. The organic rain of their dead bodies is joined by the corpses and waste products of the animals they support – from tiny filter-feeding crustaceans to fish and whales.

The decomposing particles represent life itself for bacteria and for many kinds of scavenging animal. Some, crabs and shrimps for instance, actively sift through organic debris. Others, like the sponges and giant clams, extract particles by filtering sea-water through their bodies. The microbes quickly break down much of the organic tissue into its basic chemical components; these are released back into the sea-water, from where they are taken up by the growing phytoplankton – and the cycle begins once more.

The ocean's scavengers consume nearly all organic material long before it reaches the sea floor. But besides making living tissue, a number of marine organisms also manufacture minute shells and cases from minerals extracted from the water. Some use opal, which is made of silica; others calcite, from calcium carbonate. These hard parts are not decomposed by micro-organisms, but build up as a thick ooze on the ocean floor which, after millions of years' compression and drying, will form new rock.

Individual phytoplankton cells are so small that they sink only a few slow metres per day. But velocity increases with size, and there is one process that acts as a sort of express elevator to the deep sea. The faeces of the tiny animals which graze the phytoplankton consist of waste organics, bacteria, and the hard parts of plants they have eaten. These are much larger packages, and fall faster. There is a tendency, not fully understood, for such debris to form amorphous flocs of material which sweep up smaller particles in front of them. Some flocs grow to a centimetre (.4 in) across, and are as delicate as snow-flakes; indeed, they are called 'marine snow'. Increasing in size and speed as they travel, larger particles can fall hundreds of metres per day, and material which began its life at the surface may reach the ocean floor within a matter of weeks. Such packages usually include live, active bacteria and sometimes even undecomposed phytoplankton – a rich food resource for animals struggling for survival in the ocean's barren depths.

The process by which particles form and sink, removing matter away from the surface waters, has been dubbed the 'biological pump'. It has consequences for the global environment far beyond the realm of the oceans. Through modulating the levels of carbon dioxide in the atmosphere, the biological pump influences the very climate of the planet – in the following way.

The surface oceans – some 368 million square km (nearly 141 million square miles) of water – are constantly churning, rapidly exchanging carbon dioxide with the atmosphere. Marine plants extract carbon dioxide dissolved in this way to make organic material, and 'fix' it into their tissues. Once incorporated into solid matter, carbon dioxide is carried away from the uppermost waters by the biological pump, and re-released at depth. Crucially, the carbon dioxide removed from the surface waters is immediately replaced by fresh carbon dioxide from the atmosphere. This has an important effect on atmospheric concentrations which, without the biological pump, would be three times their present level. Since global temperatures are thought to rise about 3° centigrade every time atmospheric carbon dioxide doubles, the climate would rapidly warm.

It now seems that this very effect played a major part in the climatic shifts during the ice ages. The initial triggers were probably small variations in the earth's orbit and tilt; but these alone seem unlikely to have produced such dramatic changes. This puzzled climatologists until, a few years ago, researchers found records of ancient atmospheres trapped as bubbles deep in the ice caps of Antarctica and Greenland. Analysis revealed not only that atmospheric carbon dioxide levels fluctuated hugely during the glaciations, but also that the changes occurred in exact synchrony with the waxing and waning of the ice sheets. The temperature changes appear to have been accelerated by a chain reaction involving the oceans: small climate changes caused a shift in the circulation of water in the ocean, which in turn affected the rate of the biological pump, which affected atmospheric carbon dioxide concentrations, which further altered the climate, and so on.

The oceans are necessary for the earth to support life and are, in turn, sustained by the life in them. They help to maintain the climate of the planet, which in turn must remain within certain limits – neither too cold nor too warm – for the oceans to continue to exist. In short, the oceans are part of a self-sustaining system, the whole earth system, whose different parts are dependent on the whole.

Humans too are part of this system. We have the capacity to greatly affect it, but without always knowing precisely what we are doing. We can be reasonably sure, for instance, that our burning of fossil fuels has brought to an end the million-year cycle of ice ages; but we did this before we had realized it, and we cannot predict what the consequences may be. Fortunately, we are now beginning to appreciate that our actions have truly global effects. Only by being much more vigilant in the future can we hope to maintain the health of the oceans, and ensure that they continue to play their complex role in sustaining life on earth.

---

124 A TURBAN SHELL, RED SEA

(B. Shimlock & M. Jones)

SHELLED MOLLUSCS SUCH AS THIS TURBAN SHELL ARE EXTREMELY WIDESPREAD MARINE LIFE FORMS. OPPORTUNISTS, MOLLUSCS EXPLOIT MOST FOOD SOURCES, INCLUDING ALGAL SLIME, SEAWEED, ORGANIC SEDIMENT AND DRIFTING PARTICLES, AND PLANKTON.

125

126

127

125, 126 and 127 WAVES
(Tony Stone Worldwide; Paul Berger/Tony Stone Worldwide; Warren Bolster/Tony Stone Worldwide)
CARBON DIOXIDE IN THE ATMOSPHERE DISSOLVES IN THE SEA'S CONSTANTLY
CHURNING SURFACE, TO BE TAKEN UP BY PLANT PLANKTON AND USED IN
PHOTOSYNTHESIS. DEAD PLANKTON SINK DOWN DEEP INTO THE OCEAN AS
SMALL CLUMPS. SOME ANIMAL PLANKTON ARE MIGRATING GRAZERS, THAT RISE
AT NIGHT TO FEED, THEN BY DAY DESCEND, AND RELEASE THE CARBON DIOXIDE.
THUS THE SEAS ACT AS A CARBON DIOXIDE SINK, AND ARE CONTINUALLY
DRAWING ATMOSPHERIC CARBON DIOXIDE INTO THEIR WATERS. CONSEQUENTLY,
THE AMOUNT OF THIS GAS IN THE SEAS GREATLY EXCEEDS THE AMOUNT IN THE
ATMOSPHERE. WITHOUT THIS EFFECT, ATMOSPHERIC CONCENTRATIONS WOULD
BE FAR HIGHER, AND GLOBAL TEMPERATURES WOULD SOAR.

128

128, 129 and 130   ICEBERGS, ANTARCTICA
(Ben Osborne)

WHEN A GLACIER BRINGS ICE TO THE SEA, LARGE BLOCKS BREAK OFF INTO THE
WATER, FORMING ICEBERGS. THIS PROCESS IS CALLED 'CALVING'. ONLY ABOUT
ONE NINTH OF AN ICEBERG'S TOTAL MASS PROJECTS ABOVE THE WATER. JUST AS
A RIVER CARRIES ITS HEAVIEST LOAD IN THE SPRING, SO DOES A GLACIER. THE
ICEBERG 'SEASON' OCCURS IN APRIL IN THE NORTHERN HEMISPHERE AND IN
OCTOBER IN THE SOUTHERN. BY STUDYING THE GRAVEL AND ROCKS THAT HAVE
GRADUALLY FALLEN TO THE SEABED AS ICEBERGS MELT, SCIENTISTS HAVE BEEN
ABLE TO DISCOVER THE FULL EXTENT OF ICEBERGS DURING GLACIATIONS.
GREENLAND IS THE SOURCE OF MOST OF THE ICEBERGS IN THE NORTH ATLANTIC.
THE LAST ICE AGE STARTED ABOUT 85,000 YEARS AGO AND PEAKED SOME 18,000
YEARS AGO. IT WAS THE LATEST IN A SERIES OF GLACIATIONS THAT STARTED
ABOUT ONE AND A HALF MILLION YEARS AGO. CHANGES IN THE SUN'S OUTPUT,
'GREENHOUSE' GASES, OCEANIC CIRCULATION – EVEN DUSTCLOUDS FROM
MASSIVE VOLCANIC ERUPTIONS – HAVE BEEN VARIOUSLY IMPLICATED AS CAUSES.
THE BURNING OF FOSSIL FUELS BY HUMANS MAY HAVE BROUGHT THIS CYCLE TO
AN END. WE CANNOT YET KNOW WHAT THE CONSEQUENCES WILL BE.

129

130

131

132

133

131, 132 and 133 SANDFLAT SEDIMENT (Laurie Campbell), **ACORN BARNACLES**
(Laurie Campbell), **AND URCHIN SKELETONS** (B. Jones & M. Shimlock)
SEA SHELLS ARE FORMED MAINLY OF CALCIUM CARBONATE, A MINERAL PRESENT
IN SEA-WATER, THOUGH THE SHELLS OF SOME MICROSCOPIC PLANT PLANKTON
ARE ALSO MANUFACTURED FROM SILICA. WHEN SHALLOW-WATER ANIMALS DIE,
THEIR HARD CASES ARE POUNDED INTO SEDIMENT BY THE WAVES. SIMILARLY, IN
DEEP WATER, THE SKELETONS OF MICROSCOPIC PLANT AND ANIMAL PLANKTON
ACCUMULATE INTO SEDIMENT. GRADUALLY, THEY ARE COVERED OVER BY FRESH
SEDIMENT; AFTER MILLIONS OF YEARS' COMPRESSION AND DRYING THEY WILL
FORM NEW ROCK.

134 KELP ON ROCKS AT LOW TIDE
(Kim Westerskov)
A LARGE PROPORTION OF THE
VITAL MINERALS FOUND IN SEA-
WATER ARE DERIVED FROM LAND,
ERODED FROM ROCKS BY THE
CEASELESS PASSAGE OF RIVERS
FLOWING INTO THE SEA.

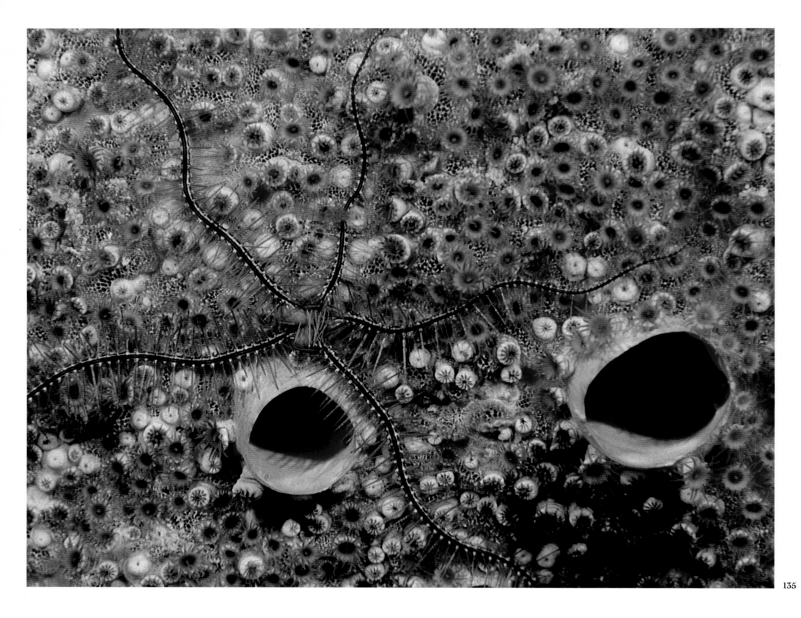

135

135 and 136 ENCRUSTING SPONGES
(J. Michael Kelly; Linda Pitkin)
SPONGES FILTER-FEED ON THE
RAIN OF SEDIMENT FROM DEAD
PLANTS AND ANIMALS LIVING AT
THE OCEAN SURFACE. THESE
PRIMITIVE ANIMALS COME IN MANY
FORMS, BUT OFTEN ENCRUST SOLID
MASSES SUCH AS REEFS AND
ROCKS.

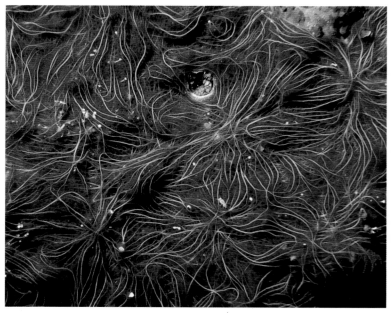

136

**137 AN AZURE VASE SPONGE,
LITTLE CAYMAN**
(David Hall)
SPONGES ARE ESSENTIALLY SIMPLE
AGGREGATIONS OF CELLS
ENCLOSING A SYSTEM OF CANALS
THROUGH WHICH WATER IS
PUMPED, BRINGING FOOD AND
OXYGEN AND REMOVING WASTE.
THEIR SHAPE IS LARGELY
GOVERNED BY THE WATER
CURRENTS WHERE THEY GROW.
WHERE WATER IS LIABLE TO MOVE
WITH FORCE, A ROUNDED CLUMP
OFFERS LESS RESISTANCE, BUT IN
TRANQUIL WATERS SHAPES MAY BE
MORE DELICATE.

139

138 A JORDAN'S PRAWN, CALIFORNIA

(Richard Herrmann)

PRAWNS OF THE *PANDALUS* SPECIES ARE BOTTOM-LIVING OMNIVORES, AND
MOVE IN LARGE SWARMS. THEY ARE MOST OFTEN FOUND ON ORGANIC-RICH
SEDIMENTS, FORAGING FOR CARRION AND PLANT DEBRIS.

139 A SPONGE CRAB, INDONESIA

(Linda Pitkin)

MOST CRABS ARE CARNIVORES AND DETRITUS-FEEDERS, SIFTING THROUGH
THE ORGANIC DEBRIS OF THE OCEAN FLOOR OR COASTLINE. SPONGE CRABS
ARE HOST TO SPONGES WHICH GROW ON THEIR SHELLS. IN THIS SYMBIOTIC
RELATIONSHIP THE CRAB ACQUIRES NOT ONLY CAMOUFLAGE BUT
PROTECTION TOO, SINCE MANY OF THE SPONGES ARE DISTASTEFUL OR
TOXIC. THE SPONGE, IN EXCHANGE, GAINS MOBILITY AND, BECAUSE CRABS
ARE MESSY EATERS, IT ALSO GETS A SHARE OF THE FOOD THE CRUSTACEAN
SCATTERS.

141

140 GOOSE BARNACLES

(IOS)

THESE SMALL CRUSTACEANS DRIFT ALONG WITH THE CURRENT, ATTACHED TO
FLOATING OBJECTS. SOME SPECIES OF GOOSE BARNACLE ATTACH THEMSELVES
TO SHIPS, AND OTHERS TO WHALES. THE LARVAE FASTEN THEMSELVES ON WITH
AN ADHESIVE SECRETED BY A 'CEMENT GLAND', AND WITHIN JUST TEN DAYS
THEY HAVE MATURED. WITH THEIR FROND-LIKE TENTACLES, THEY CATCH
WHATEVER COMES THEIR WAY, SCAVENGING PLANT AND ANIMAL FRAGMENTS
FROM THE WATER.

141 FAN-WORMS, CARIBBEAN

(Norbert Wu)

FAN-WORMS LIVE IN COLONIES ATTACHED TO ROCKS AND CORAL. THEIR BODIES
END IN A CROWN OF FAN-LIKE FRONDS, WHICH FILTER FINE PARTICLES
INCLUDING PLANKTON FROM THE WATER BUT ALSO SERVE AS THE ANIMALS'
GILLS. THE CROWNS RAPIDLY CONTRACT IF TOUCHED.

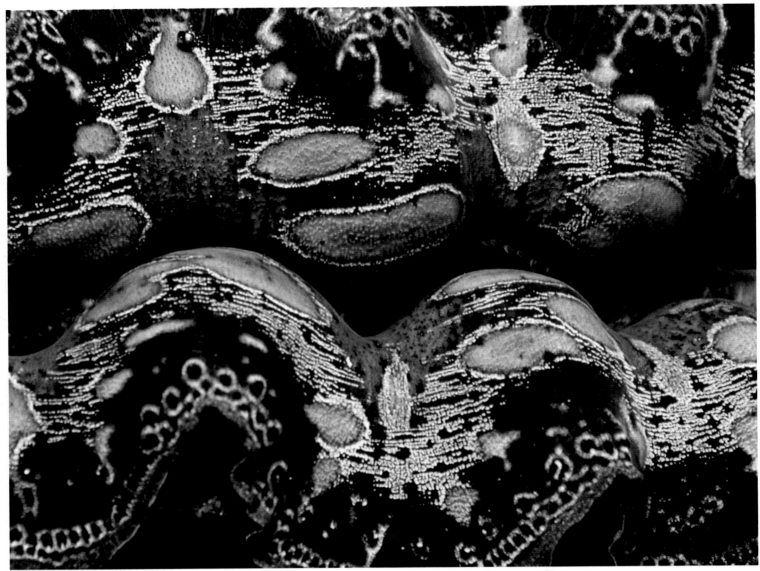

142

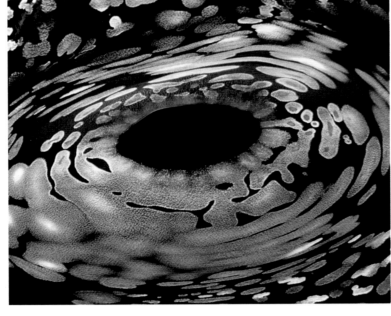

143

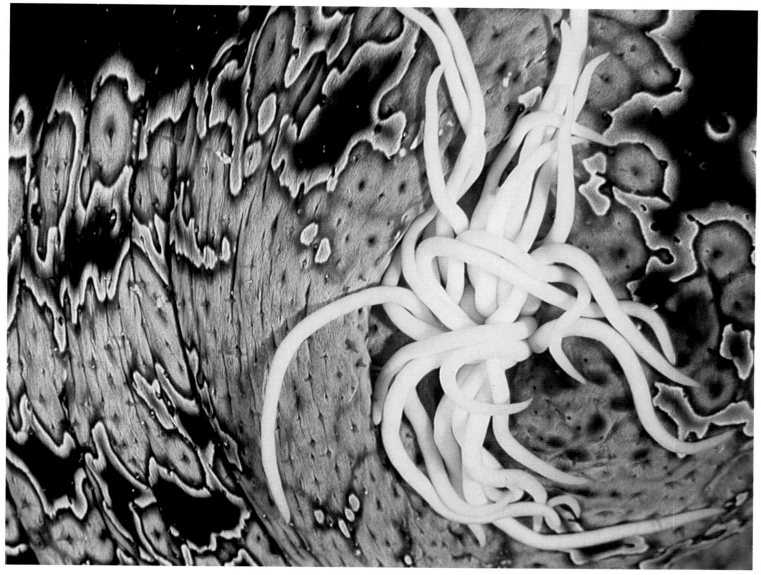

144

142 and 143   **THE GIANT CLAM: DETAIL OF A MANTLE** (David Hall),
AND A SYPHON (David Hall)
FORMERLY WIDESPREAD IN TROPICAL WATERS, GIANT CLAMS ARE NOW
THREATENED BY HUMANS HUNTING THEM FOR THEIR FLESH AND THEIR SHELLS.
THEY GROW UP TO A METRE (3 FT) IN DIAMETER. CLAMS FEED BY EXTRACTING
ORGANIC PARTICLES FROM THE WATER THAT THEY SIPHON THROUGH THEIR
MOUTHPARTS. PHOTOSYNTHESIZING ALGAE LIVE IN THEIR MANTLES, AND
PROVIDE THEM WITH ADDITIONAL ENERGY.

144   **A SEA CUCUMBER EVISCERATING, FIJI**
(B. Jones & M. Shimlock)
SEA CUCUMBERS ARE A LARGE GROUP OF SOFT, SAUSAGE-SHAPED ANIMALS THAT
FEED ON DEBRIS AMONG THE MUD OR SAND OF THE SEA FLOOR, WHERE MOST
SPECIES LIVE. WHEN ATTACKED, THEY SOMETIMES EVISCERATE, OR THROW OUT
THEIR INTERNAL ORGANS, WHICH ARE STICKY, AND DISTASTEFUL TO THE
PREDATOR. THE ORGANS REGENERATE.

145

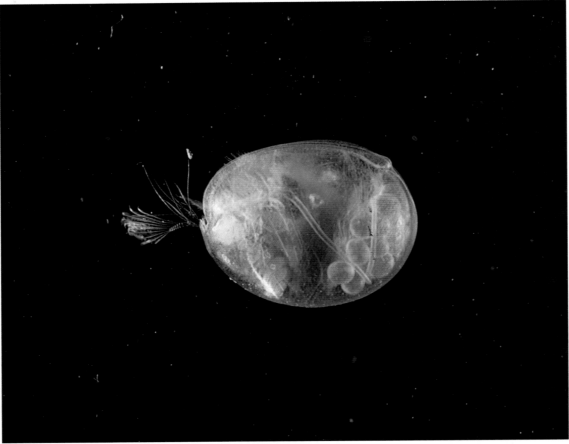

146

145 and 146   A LUMINOUS SEA CUCUMBER (IOS), **AND A FEMALE OSTRACOD, WITH EGGS** (IOS)
BOTH OF THESE DEEP-SEA CREATURES LIVE OFF THE DEBRIS LEFT BEHIND AFTER MORE SHALLOW-WATER ANIMALS HAVE FINISHED SCAVENGING. THOUGH IT IS SOMETIMES FOUND CLOSER TO THE SURFACE, THIS SEA CUCUMBER IS AT HOME AT DEPTHS OF 5,000 METRES (OVER 3 MILES). THE SYMBIOTIC BACTERIA THAT INHABIT ITS TENTACLES MAY HELP IT TO DIGEST FOOD. THE OSTRACOD, A SMALL CRUSTACEAN, LIVES AT DEPTHS OF 3,000 METRES (ALMOST 2 MILES) AND MORE. THE PINK BALLS VISIBLE HERE ARE ITS EGGS.

147   THE DEEP-SEA CRUSTACEAN, *EURYTHENES GRYLLUS*
(IOS)
THE 'BLUEBOTTLE' OF THE OCEANS: IT AVIDLY DEVOURS CORPSES AND OTHER DEBRIS THAT SINK TO THE SEA FLOOR WHERE IT LIVES.

CHAPTER EIGHT

MOVING MOUNTAINS:
THE DYNAMIC OCEAN FLOOR
SIR ANTHONY LAUGHTON

Sea-water conceals two thirds of the world's surface, so that few of us will ever see some of the most dramatic scenery on earth. The great mountain ranges, vast trenches and enormous plains of the deep ocean floor have been moulded by literally earth-shattering events – earthquakes, landslides, volcanic explosions and more – which have taken place, for the most part unheard and unseen, over hundreds of millions of years.

THE CONTOURS OF THE SEA FLOOR, AND CONSEQUENTLY of the entire planet, are in constant flux. To explore the landscape beneath the sea is to understand the dynamism and endlessly changing nature of the earth itself.

Imagine a tour of this submarine landscape. Beyond the sea's familiar shores, a great continental shelf, carved from the land over millennia by the ocean's eroding forces, stretches out for perhaps 200 km (around 150 miles). It gives way finally to a slope many tens of kilometres long, cut with canyons and so steep that it would be hard to ride a bicycle up it. At its base, over 3 km (2 miles) below sea level, lies a thick accumulation of sediment, sometimes spreading for a hundred kilometres or more, washed down from the slope and the land above. This marks the true edge of the continent, and the beginning of the vast basins which represent over 90 per cent of the world's oceans.

Beyond, a perfectly flat or gently undulating expanse of sand and mud extends as far as the eye can see, disturbed only by the tracks and burrows of bottom-living animals. Occasionally, though, hills and mountains arise from these abyssal plains, thickly coated in a pale, chalky ooze. These deposits, bizarrely

---

148 DURDLE DOOR, DORSET, ENGLAND
(David Noton)
OVER VAST TIME SCALES, THE SEA DISCOVERS WEAKNESSES IN THE JOINTS AND
FISSURES OF ROCKS, AND CARVES A MAGNIFICENT COASTLINE OF HEADLANDS,
CAVES AND ARCHES.

reminiscent of snow, are the decomposing remains of plankton which have rained down from the surface waters far above.

As we progress still further away from the continent, the terrain becomes increasingly rugged. Lava flows which have poured from deep fissures in the ocean crust form frozen lakes; others have been squeezed from narrow openings like toothpaste from a tube. There are precipitous mountains thrust upwards by faults a kilometre (over half a mile) high, and huge ravines where the earth's crust is being pulled apart by forces 150 km (100 miles) below.

Towards the centre of the ocean basins rise the foothills of the largest mountain range in the world. The mid-ocean ridge – comprising the Mid-Atlantic Ridge, Mid-Indian Ocean Ridge, and East Pacific Rise – winds through the world's oceans to form an almost continuous chain some 56,000 km (35,000 miles) long. Its tallest peaks break through the sea's surface to form the islands of the Azores; further north, the ridge penetrates again, as Iceland.

Exploring this mountainous realm, we may encounter what look strangely like tall plumes of black smoke billowing from fractures, sometimes many kilometres deep, in the ocean floor. Water entering these hydrothermal vents is heated by the furnace-like rocks within to 300° centigrade or more; from there it shoots out in great jets, cooling rapidly on contact with the surrounding sea. The water is coloured black by chemical particles dissolved from the hot rocks: sulphides of tin, silver, copper and zinc, which build up as brittle chimney-like structures around the vents.

Incredibly, clustered around these openings are a bizarre assembly of living things: bright-red, mouthless giant tubeworms, giant clams and hitherto unknown species of crabs. Such creatures contradict all conventional laws of nature, since they derive no energy, directly or indirectly, from the sun. Instead, these miniature ecosystems are supported by bacteria that synthesize energy from sulphur discharged by the vents.

In the Pacific Ocean, travelling westwards away from the East Pacific Rise, we find an entirely new landscape. Barely 150 kilometres from land on the west Pacific margin, the depth increases dramatically as we plunge into the great oceanic trenches. These long, narrow depressions are bordered by volcanic island arcs such as Japan, the Philippines and the Marianas. The Marianas Trench is the deepest yet discovered, plunging at its lowest point some 11,000 metres (nearly 7 miles) below sea level.

How, and when, did these sea-floor features form, and what do they tell us about the history of the earth? One discovery in the 1950s helped to unlock the puzzle. Marine geologists found that the sediments accumulated over oceanic rocks became progressively older the further away from the mid-ocean ridges they appeared. The oldest rocks in the oceans are just 200 million years or so, whereas the oldest ones on the continents are put at nearly *4,000* million. Scientists realized that the planet's surface, far from being static, is extremely mobile.

The globe's crust is broken into at least twelve large, rigid plates, which compose its outer shell. Driven by motions of the underlying mantle, these plates are constantly, if slowly, moving towards or away from one another. While they themselves are relatively stable, their boundaries are zones of intense volcanic and earthquake activity, and it is here that the mid-ocean ridges arise. Molten magma from the earth's fiery, viscous mantle breaks through the thin crust and spews on to the floor, creating vast mountain ranges. With each eruption, the new crust spreads wider, forcing the plates and the older crust ever further back. Hence younger, exclusively volcanic rocks are found towards the ridges, while older ones, covered by other sediments, are found the further away we go.

In this way, the ocean itself expands, growing at about the same rate as a fingernail – between 2.5 and 25 cm (1 and 10 in) a year. But not every sea floor can be expanding, or the earth as a whole would be getting bigger; instead, the spreading of some ocean areas is balanced by the shrinking of others. This explains the great belt of trenches found in the western Pacific; here, the oceanic crust has been forced back down into the earth's interior. These enormous forces generate the deep earthquakes of the region, while some of the now molten rock rises to form the volcanoes of the island arcs. But much of the swallowed rock will be conveyed back to the region below the mid-ocean ridges, to erupt and be re-processed once more. It seems likely that the ocean crust has been recycled in this way many times throughout the planet's history, though each circulation takes hundreds of millions of years.

The map of the world today looks very different from the way it did even fifty million years ago, for the spreading sea floor also pushes continents away from one another. In time, drifting continents may collide with other landmasses, and the crust between them may be squeezed upwards to appear above the sea. This is happening now, as Africa moves northwards to collide with Europe; the crust which has already emerged now forms part of Crete. The Troodos Massif of Cyprus arose in a similar way: the ancient ocean floor can be seen in sediments of mudstone, chalk and limestone, reefs built on the sediment, strangely formed pillow lavas, and the crystallized residue of the magma chamber itself.

When all the ocean crust between converging plates has been swallowed, the continents collide. Sometimes this thrusts their edges upwards as mountain ranges. The Himalayas are the youngest mountains to have been formed in this way: they arose when the Indian continent drifted north away from Antarctica and, about ten million years ago, joined with Asia. The collision lifted the landmass and its continental shelf 8 km (5 miles) high; the old sea floor, embedded with marine fossils, now lies on the mountain tops.

Older mountain chains formed in the same way have already been eroded by frost, rain and wind, and are sometimes only recognizable by their roots. Such ranges may be created and destroyed in a matter of tens of millions of years, and the Himalayas themselves are already being attacked; the great rivers of the Indus and the Ganges are heavy with their sediments, which accumulate as thick basins in the northern Arabian Sea and the Bay of Bengal.

At the edge of the continental shelves, such sediments can build up as huge, precariously balanced deposits. If destabilized by an earthquake the sediment may begin to slide down the continental slope, gathering speed and increasing in density as it descends. These turbidity currents may travel at 80 km (50 miles) an hour, flattening everything in their path to form the enormous abyssal plains which abut many of the continental shelves. Destabilized sediments can also trigger massive underwater landslides. Seven thousand years ago, the Storegga slide west of Norway moved chunks of the continental slope 15 km (10 miles) wide and hurled them 150 km away, causing a tidal wave which flooded the east coast of Scotland. Catastrophic submarine landslides and turbidity currents may occur several times in a century, though most go unnoticed and unrecorded. However, their impact on sea-floor life can be dramatic, and it may be hundreds of years before the ecosystem is re-established.

Thus even the ocean's rocks are impermanent and are constantly being recycled, albeit on an immense time scale. Many of the features and processes involved have only recently been understood, and still more recently accepted by the scientific establishment. But only a small fraction of the ocean floor has been explored in detail. Much more remains to be discovered about this vast, ancient, yet dynamic realm, whose great cycles shape and influence not just the marine environment, but the land on which we live.

---

149   A RIVER OF MOLTEN LAVA, KILAUEA RIFT, HAWAII

(Soames Summerhays/Biofotos)

VOLCANIC ACTIVITY SHAPES MANY OF THE WORLD'S LANDSCAPES, BOTH ABOVE
AND BELOW THE SEA. THE HAWAIIAN ISLANDS ARE FORMED IN THIS WAY, WHILE
UNDERSEA VOLCANOES HAVE BUILT THE GREAT MID-OCEAN RIDGE – THE
LARGEST MOUNTAIN RANGE ON EARTH.

150

151

150   THE GIANT'S CAUSEWAY, COUNTY ANTRIM, NORTHERN IRELAND
(Heather Angel)
REGULAR GEOMETRIC LAVA FORMATIONS OCCUR WHEN GREAT THICKNESSES OF MOLTEN BASALT FROM A VOLCANIC ERUPTION COOL VERY SLOWLY. THE GIANT'S CAUSEWAY CONSISTS OF THOUSANDS OF COLUMNS, MOST OF THEM HEXAGONAL, FORMING A STAIRCASE DOWN TO THE SEA.

151   A HYDROTHERMAL VENT, GALAPAGOS RIFT, PACIFIC OCEAN
(Robert Hessler/Planet Earth)
DEEP DOWN ON THE OCEAN FLOOR AT THE CREST OF THE MID-OCEAN RIDGE, FISSURES IN THE EARTH'S CRUST ALLOW THE SEA-WATER TO CIRCULATE AND TO HEAT UP. THE HOT WATER THAT EMERGES FROM THE SEA FLOOR, FORCED UP BY CONVECTION, IS LADEN WITH CHEMICALS THAT PRECIPITATE AS BLACK PARTICLES. THESE 'BLACK SMOKERS', OR HYDROTHERMAL VENTS, SUPPORT AN ENTIRE MINI-ECOSYSTEM TEEMING WITH CRABS, TUBE WORMS, MOLLUSCS AND MORE – WHICH FLY IN THE FACE OF NATURE, DEPENDING ON CHEMICALS FOR LIFE RATHER THAN SUNLIGHT.

152

152   KILAUEA VOLCANO, HAWAII
(Bob Cranston/Norbert Wu Photography)
THE HAWAIIAN CHAIN CONSISTS OF A SERIES OF VOLCANIC ISLANDS FORMED AS
THE EARTH'S CRUST BENEATH THE PACIFIC OCEAN MOVES NORTHWESTWARD
OVER AN ABNORMALLY HOT ZONE IN THE EARTH'S UPPER MANTLE, AND LIQUID
MAGMA IS FORCED UP THROUGH IT. KILAUEA VOLCANO, ON THE ISLAND OF
HAWAII AT THE SOUTHEAST END OF THE CHAIN, IS THE YOUNGEST AND ONE OF
THE MOST ACTIVE VOLCANOES IN THE WORLD.

153

154

153 and 155 STAIR HOLE, DORSET
(Heather Angel), **AND CLIFFS,
CORNWALL** (Heather Angel)
TECTONIC PLATE MOVEMENT AND
VOLCANIC ACTIVITY MAKE THE
EARTH'S CRUST EXPAND AND
SPREAD, THRUSTING SOME PARTS
OF IT UP ABOVE THE SEA OR BACK
DOWN INTO THE EARTH'S
INTERIOR. THE ACUTE FOLDING
SEEN IN STAIR HOLE IS THE RESULT
OF SUCH PRESSURE. LAYERS OF
ROCK THAT ONCE FORMED THE
OCEAN FLOOR CAN BE SEEN
DEFORMED AND NOW EXPOSED.
THE CORNISH CLIFFS, SEEN HERE,
SHOW A SIMILAR FOLDING.

**154 SANDFLATS, NORTH UIST,
SCOTLAND**
(Laurie Campbell)
FLATS OF MUD OR SAND FORM
ALONGSIDE MOST OF THE
ESTUARIES OF THE WORLD, THEIR
AREAS EXTENDING OR
DIMINISHING ACCORDING TO THE
TIDES. SEDIMENT BORNE BY RIVERS
EMPTIES INTO THE SEAS'
ESTUARINE BASINS; THE TIDE THEN
RETURNS SOME OF THESE
DEPOSITS TO THE LAND, FORMING
SANDFLATS.

155

156

156 and 157   WARREN POINT, DEVON (David Noton), **AND POINT OF STOER,**
SUTHERLAND, SCOTLAND (David Noton)

THE VARIOUS MINERAL STRUCTURES OF ROCKS DETERMINE COASTLINE
FORMATIONS. AFTER MILLIONS OF YEARS OF WEATHERING BY SEA AND WIND,
ONLY THE MORE RESISTANT SUBSTANCES REMAIN. GRANITE AND CERTAIN
LIMESTONES YIELD ONLY SLOWLY, BUT THE SEA UNDERCUTS EVEN THESE,
CARVING OUT STACKS AND CAVES, ARCHES AND CLIFFS. WITH THE RELENTLESS
POUNDING OF THE WAVES, SOFTER ROCKS CRUMBLE AWAY, AND THE DEBRIS IS
WASHED ALONG THE COAST TO CREATE BEACHES AND PEBBLE BANKS.

158

158, 159 and 160   SEABIRDS ON ROUGH SEAS, AUCKLAND ISLAND, NEW ZEALAND
(Kim Westerskov), **ISLAY, SCOTLAND** (Laurie Campbell), **AND BIG SISTER ISLAND,**
NEW ZEALAND (Kim Westerskov/OSF)
DRAMATIC CLIFFS ARE FORMED WHERE ROUGH SEAS, CAUSED BY DISTANT AS
WELL AS LOCAL STORMS, POUND AT THE BASE. THE WAVES CARRY AWAY LOOSE
OR WEAKENED ROCK, AND HURL FRAGMENTS AGAINST THE FACE. WAVES CAN
EVEN COMPRESS AIR INTO THE ROCKS' JOINTS, SO THAT WHEN THEY RETREAT
THE AIR EXPLODES. STORM WAVES EXERT PRESSURE UP TO 30 TONNES PER
SQUARE METRE – ENOUGH TO DEFEAT THE MOST RESILIENT ROCKS.

159

160

161

161 AN ATOLL FORMING: HERON ISLAND, GREAT BARRIER REEF, QUEENSLAND
(Gerry Ellis)
AN ATOLL IS A CORAL REEF IN THE SHAPE OF A RING OR A HORSESHOE,
ENCLOSING A LAGOON. ACCORDING TO DARWIN, AN ATOLL BEGINS TO FORM
WHEN A CORAL FRINGE GROWS AROUND A VOLCANIC ISLAND. THE LOAD WHICH
THE VOLCANO IMPOSES ON THE EARTH'S CRUST MAKES IT BEND UNDER THE
WEIGHT, AND SO THE ISLAND BEGINS TO SINK. THE CORAL, THOUGH, GROWS
FASTER THAN THE ISLAND SINKS, RESULTING IN A CORAL RING SURROUNDING A
LAGOON. MOST ATOLLS ARE FOUND IN THE PACIFIC OCEAN. THEY FORM THE
ISLAND SYSTEM OF MICRONESIA, IN THE INDIAN OCEAN, THE MALDIVES AND THE
LACCADIVES. ATOLLS MAY RANGE IN SIZE FROM LESS THAN A KILOMETRE TO
OVER 120 KM (75 MILES) IN DIAMETER, AND ARE VERY LOW-LYING. BECAUSE OF
THIS, EVEN SMALL RISES IN SEA LEVEL MAKE THEM VERY VULNERABLE TO
FLOODING.

162   THE BEACH BELOW MOUNT SANTUBONG, SARAWAK
(Heather Angel)
WASHED DOWN FROM THE LAND BY RIVERS, ERODED SEDIMENT ACCUMULATES
IN THE COASTAL ZONE – SEEN HERE AS THE DARKER WAVY BANDS ALONG THE
TIDEMARK. THIS PROCESS IS THE SOURCE OF MANY OF THE MINERALS FOUND
DISSOLVED IN SEA-WATER. THE LARGER GRAINS OF SEDIMENT FIND THEIR WAY
INTO THE DEEP OCEAN BASINS, FORMING THE MASSIVE ACCUMULATIONS OF
SEDIMENT AT THE FOOT OF THE CONTINENTAL SLOPE.

162

164

163   CORAL ISLANDS, PALAU, MICRONESIA

(David Hall)

WHEN ISLANDS ARE FORMED, THE FIRST LIFE TO COLONIZE THE NEW LAND
IS NOT ALWAYS PLANTS. FIRST MAY COME INSECTS AND SMALL ORGANISMS
THAT FEED ON CARRION WASHED UP ON THE SHORE. BOTH PLANTS AND
ANIMAL ORGANISMS ARE OFTEN FIRST BROUGHT BY SEABIRDS.

164   A CORAL LAGOON, FIJI

(Norbert Wu)

LAGOONS ARE WARM, SHALLOW, QUIET WATERWAYS SEPARATED FROM THE
OPEN SEA BY SANDBARS, BARRIER ISLANDS OR CORAL REEFS, OR A
COMBINATION OF THESE. CORAL ATOLLS ENCLOSE ROUGHLY CIRCULAR
LAGOONS, WHICH THEMSELVES ARE ALSO CORAL-BOTTOMED, LIKE THE ONE
SHOWN HERE. THE PALM TREES FRINGING THE LAGOON ARE TYPICAL CORAL
ISLAND VEGETATION.

CHAPTER NINE

LIFE ON THE EDGE:
A MOSAIC OF ECOSYSTEMS
DR NICHOLAS POLUNIN

Looking down from a plane, or battling against the surf on an open beach, we are struck by the contrast between land and sea. Within a few metres the familiar terrestrial greens and browns, the reassuringly solid earth, give way to shades of blue, shifting footholds, the swirl and surge of water – and whatever may lurk below. But the coast is not only a boundary; it is its own domain, which in turn encompasses a mosaic of ecosystems.

COASTAL HABITATS – SALT MARSHES, ESTUARIES, MUD-flats, sand dunes, temperate rocky shores, tropical man-groves, coral reefs, seagrass meadows and kelp forests – are each host to a community of organisms uniquely adapted to that particular environment.

But no marine habitat exists in isolation from the rest; the life cycles of plants and animals make for constant interaction between one part of the ocean and another, and here at the margins the traffic is particularly intense. The special conditions of certain coastal environments, protected and rich in food, support not only permanent residents but also numerous visitors that normally inhabit the open ocean. Many sea fish – the Atlantic herring, for instance – spawn in coastal waters; turtles return from the deep sea to hatching beaches to lay their eggs; even the great whales calve in sheltered tropical bays. While much of the open ocean is sparsely populated, the seas close to land seethe with life. So prolific are they that over three quarters of marine fishery production derives from coastal waters, though they form just a tenth of the oceans' entire area.

Why should the coasts be so rich in life? In fact, not all coastal environments are so productive, and different factors

---

165 A GIANT KELP, CALIFORNIA

(Georgette Douwma/Planet Earth)

WHOLE FORESTS OF THESE TOWERING SEAWEEDS GROW IN THE COOLER PARTS

OF THE PACIFIC. THIS ONE, *MACROCYSTIS PYRIFERA*, IS THE GIANT OF THEM ALL,

CAPABLE OF LIVING AT DEPTHS OF 30 METRES (100 FT) OR MORE.

influence those that are. The key, as so often, is the availability of nutrients needed by the plankton, algae, and other ocean plants which are the basis of all marine ecosystems. Tropical waters, for example, tend to be poor in nutrients; but in some areas, such as the coast of Peru, atmosphere and ocean interact to bring deep nutrient-rich water welling to the surface. This stimulates plankton production, which supports a huge variety of fish life; and the fish attract birds, which are seen in burgeoning populations along the coast.

Estuaries, meanwhile, are biologically rich habitats for different reasons. River waters thick with the accumulations of upland peats, lowland swamps and plant debris of all kinds pour into the oceans; each year, they shed an estimated 400 million tonnes of organic matter into the sea. These swirling sediments provide food for plankton and marine creatures, and especially for the swarms of larvae from the many fish and crustaceans that breed in estuarine waters.

A surprisingly multifarious animal life populates the apparently empty brown stretches of tropical and temperate mud-flats which often form near estuaries. A myriad uniquely adapted species thrive beneath the organic ooze. Moon snails plough through the silt; clams lurk in the mud with only their siphons visible; assorted crab species live in, under or alongside the flats. Huge numbers of tiny invertebrates wriggle among the particles of mud and sand; in the Gulf of Maine, over a thousand species were found inhabiting one small bay. Theirs is a secret, muddy world, yet one which presents a cornucopia to numerous shore birds – oyster-catchers, for example, or sand-pipers – which forage industriously over the flats.

In the tropics, some salt marshes and muddy tidal estuaries are colonized by mangrove forests. Mangroves are formed by *Rhizophora*, the only trees able to flourish in salt water, their woody stilt-like roots repeatedly submerged and exposed by the tides. These trap dead leaves and sediment and provide a murky, nutrient-rich underwater environment for oysters, shrimps, crabs, sponges, jellyfish and many indigenous fish, as well as a hospitable nursery for the young of ocean-living fish such as sharks, mullet and tarpon. Red and blue fiddler crabs pick through the mud, and pop-eyed carnivorous mudskippers search out prey. Frigate birds, pelicans and herons roost in the trees.

But mangroves also serve a wider function, for they build new land. The sediment which accretes in their roots is invaded and bound by new plants; as the mangrove encroaches ever further into the sea, the oldest forest is gradually colonized by terrestrial plants. The Florida Bay Keys, for example, are a tribute to mangrove land-building.

Close to shore, the sandy floors of tropical seas such as the Caribbean are strewn with grass meadows. Amongst their blades live minute crustaceans, which attract schools of tiny, darting fish. Occasionally, they are joined by the rare and endangered manatee, or sea cow. These large, leisurely, gentle animals may weigh up to 800 kg (1,760 lb) and are the only exclusively vegetarian marine mammals. The females sometimes hold their young to their breasts when nursing on the water's surface, and probably inspired the mermaid legends.

But for variety of life forms and luxuriance of colour, no habitat can match the tropical coral reefs – the most biologically diverse environments on earth. Elkhorn, pillar, mountain, brain, moon, finger and fire are just a few kinds of coral, their names announcing the immense variety of their sizes and shapes. Corals are tiny tentacled animals that filter-feed from the water, but they also obtain energy from the photosynthesizing algae, or zooxanthellae, that live symbiotically in their tissues. It is the zooxanthellae that help stony corals to manufacture their limestone skeletons which, over thousands of years, accumulate to form great reefs. Many stretch for hundreds of kilometres; the largest known coral complex, the Great Barrier Reef off northeast Australia, is upwards of 1,600 km (1,000 miles) long and 150 km (90 miles) across at its widest point. It contains over 200 species of coral alone.

Reef topography, featuring dramatic hills, dark caves, plateaux and valleys, can be breathtaking. Pinnacles loom, festooned with fish; tunnels disappear into the coral, their entrances ringed with sea-fans. Then, suddenly, comes a sheer cliff – and the resounding, empty blue of the ocean.

In the reef waters, and seemingly in every cave, corner and crevice, live a vast and exotic array of animals. A thousand species of fish may be found on just one reef in the eastern Pacific, not to mention the invertebrates – clams, cowries, slugs and snails, starfish and urchins, anemones, crabs, shrimps and lobsters. In these intensely crowded ecosystems, each animal competes with its neighbour for food, for mates, for sheer space. Such conditions produce unlikely associations. Shrimps and brilliantly coloured clown-fish live among the stinging tentacles of anemones. Tiny 'cleaner' fish feed by ridding the bodies of larger fish of harmful parasites; even species that usually prey on each other declare a truce while the cleaner fish performs its services.

In nearshore temperate seas, complex and spectacular environments are also provided by the large seaweeds known as kelps. Small varieties like the furbelows, sea tangles and sea lace grow off the rocky Atlantic and North Sea coasts. In the cooler parts of the Pacific, kelps reach gigantic proportions, their branching stems, or 'stipes', extending for 30 metres (100 ft) or more. Seaweeds absorb nutrients from the surrounding water and have no need of roots; kelps anchor themselves to the seabed with 'holdfasts' which may be a metre (over 3 ft) across, enabling them to withstand the constant buffeting they endure.

In these underwater forests, the kelps are the 'trees', the fish and marine mammals the 'birds'. In the 'branches' and among the 'roots' live distinct communities of animals. The branching holdfasts of horsetail kelps, for example, form arched columns which are home to mussels and sea-squirts, starfish and urchins. The kelp blades are colonized by lacy, plant-like animals called bryozoans, and by a multitude of tiny micro-organisms. Large-shelled abalone – the favourite food of visiting sea otters – swim amongst fishes such as the gaudy orange garibaldi, the sheepshead, and the ugly cabezon. Passing visitors to these rich hunting grounds include whales, seals – even the great white shark.

Further inland, the rugged shores of temperate coasts display an astounding variety of life forms. Each is geared to the harsh environment of the wave-pounded tidal zone, much of which is submerged only at high tide. In the most landward fringe, periwinkles graze on lichens and algae, and barnacles crowd the rocks. Crabs scuttle about in search of dinner, themselves in danger of becoming a meal for the gulls which wheel and cry above. Further towards the sea, rock pools are adorned with elegant plumose anemones, next to fiercely clinging starfish and purple urchins, competing for footholds with chitons and limpets. Blue-black mussels cluster; dog-whelks, their predators, nestle in rocky hollows. A wide array of seaweeds grow anywhere they can, providing a moist, sheltering blanket for other organisms when the tide is out.

Thus the coasts furnish a vast range of habitats, more dense in life than anything in the open ocean. But they are also a focus for human beings. Today, more people are concentrated along the narrow coastal strip than any other place in the world, and the environment inevitably suffers. Pollution is a hazard to many life forms, and is particularly dangerous here since enclosed coastal waters cannot easily cleanse themselves. Over-fishing destroys the balance of these fragile ecosystems and has implications for the entire marine habitat, since many species begin their lives here. In short, it is at the ocean's margins that we face the greatest environmental challenge.

---

166 A PAIR OF ALBATROSSES, AUSTRALIA

(Graham Robertson)

THE ROCKY COASTS OF TEMPERATE AND POLAR REGIONS PROVIDE NESTING

GROUNDS FOR VAST NUMBERS OF SEABIRDS, INCLUDING ALBATROSSES.

168

167 and 169 A CHINSTRAP PENGUIN
CHICK HATCHES (Ben Osborne), AND
AN EMPEROR CHICK NESTLES ON
ITS PARENT'S FEET (Kim Westerskov)
FEMALE PENGUINS LAY THEIR
SINGLE WHITE EGGS IN MAY OR
JUNE. FOR THE WHOLE OF THE
SIXTY DAYS' INCUBATION, DURING
THE COLDEST PART OF THE
ANTARCTIC WINTER, THE MALE
EMPEROR STANDS WITH HIS EGG
ON HIS FEET, TUCKED UNDER A
FATTY FOLD OF SKIN TO KEEP IT
WARM. THE FEMALE, WHICH HAS
BEEN AWAY FEEDING AT SEA,
RETURNS ON HATCHING DAY, THEN
FEEDS THE CHICK. NOW CARE
ROLES ARE REVERSED, AND THE
MALE GOES OFF IN SEARCH OF THE
OPEN SEA AND A SQUARE MEAL.

169

168 KING PENGUINS, WITH CHICKS
(Gerry Ellis)
THE BROWN, FLUFFY FLEDGLINGS
ARE ONE YEAR OLD – PENNED IN
BY THE ADULTS IN THIS WAY, THEY
ARE LESS VULNERABLE TO
PREDATORS. COLONIES USUALLY
NUMBER 20,000-60,000 BIRDS. KING
PENGUIN CHICKS MATURE FOR A
FULL YEAR ON LAND – LONGER
THAN ANY OTHER SPECIES –
FEEDING ON KRILL REGURGITATED
BY THEIR PARENTS, BEFORE THEY
GO TO SEA FOR THE FIRST TIME.

170 ROYAL ALBATROSSES NESTING, MIDDLE SISTER ISLAND
(Kim Westerskov)
ALBATROSSES SPEND MANY MONTHS ON THE COLD SOUTHERN SEA, COMING ASHORE ONLY TO BREED, USUALLY ON WINDSWEPT ISLANDS FAR FROM HUMAN HABITATION. ROYAL ALBATROSSES BREED EVERY TWO YEARS, AND THE EGG TAKES UP TO THREE MONTHS TO INCUBATE. ONCE HATCHED, THE CHICK MAY STAY IN THE NEST FOR A YEAR.

171

172

**171 and 172   A GANNET COLONY,
BRITAIN** (Richard Matthews/Planet Earth),
**AND BLUE-EYED SHAGS WITH
THEIR CHICKS, ANTARCTICA** (Ben
Osborne)
THE NORTHERN GANNET LIVES IN
LARGE, NOISY COLONIES ALONG
COASTS, AND FORAGES IN THE SEA,
MAKING FREQUENT COMPLEX
DISPLAYS TO DO WITH PAIR-
BONDING AND SITE OWNERSHIP. AT
NESTING TIME GANNETS ARE AT
THEIR MOST AGGRESSIVE. IF AN
ADULT BIRD LANDS AT THE WRONG
NEST, OR IF A CHICK STRAYS INTO
ANOTHER'S TERRITORY, THE
OFFENDER MAY BE PECKED TO
DEATH. SHAGS, TOO, ARE
VIGOROUS IN DEFENCE OF THEIR
NESTS AND YOUNG.

173   A KITTIWAKE AT ITS NEST
(Laurie Campbell)
KITTIWAKES CONGREGATE IN
LARGE COLONIES ON NARROW
CLIFF EDGES AND GULLIES. THEY
SECURE THEIR NESTS WITH
SEAWEED, WHICH ADHERES TO THE
ROCK AS IT DRIES. ABOUT HALF A
MILLION PAIRS BREED IN BRITAIN
AND IRELAND. ONCE SLAUGHTERED
FOR SPORT AND TO PROVIDE
FEATHERS FOR WOMEN'S HATS, THE
KITTIWAKE IS NOW A PROTECTED
SPECIES.

173

174

174   TWO GIANT SPINED STARFISH, POINT LOBOS, MONTEREY, CALIFORNIA
(Norbert Wu)
THE INTERTIDAL ZONE OF TEMPERATE COASTS IS OFTEN HOST TO STARFISH LIKE
THESE GIANTS, WELL ADAPTED TO THE RIGOURS OF EXPOSURE WHEN THE TIDE
IS OUT, AS IT IS HERE. MOST STARFISH HAVE FIVE ARMS, BUT SOME SPECIES HAVE
UP TO TWENTY-FIVE. EACH ARM CONTAINS AN EXTENSION OF THE BODY CAVITY
AND ORGANS. THE NUMEROUS PLATES UNDER THE SKIN, WHICH FORM THE
EXOSKELETON, ARE LINKED BY MUSCLE AND CONNECTIVE TISSUE, GIVING THE
APPARENTLY RIGID CREATURE CONSIDERABLE FLEXIBILITY. STARFISH AND MANY
OTHER ANIMALS TAKE REFUGE AMONGST THE WET POOLS AND TRAILING WEEDS
WHICH ARE ALSO CHARACTERISTIC OF THE INTERTIDAL ZONE.

175 SURF GRASS, TORREY PINES STATE PARK, CALIFORNIA, AT LOW TIDE

(Richard Herrmann)

MANY COASTAL SEAWEEDS ARE EXPOSED AT LOW TIDE, PROVIDING A
COMFORTABLY WET SHELTER FOR SMALL ANIMALS SUCH AS SHELLFISH, WHICH
MIGHT OTHERWISE DIE FROM DESICCATION. ON THE SANDY SEA FLOORS OFF THE
WEST COAST OF AMERICA, AND IN THE CARIBBEAN, GRASSES PROLIFERATE.
SUBMERGED AT HIGH TIDE, THEY RESEMBLE UNDERWATER MEADOWS. AND, LIKE
THEIR TERRESTRIAL COUNTERPARTS, THEY ARE SOMETIMES OVER-GRAZED BY
THE CREATURES THAT FEED ON THEM. SEA URCHINS, FOR INSTANCE, OFTEN
NIBBLE SO CLOSE TO THE ROOTS THAT THE PLANTS DIE OFF. BUT ALGAE MAY
SPRING UP ON PATCHES OF BARE SAND, AND IN TIME THE GRASSES RETURN.

176

177

178

176 and 177   **SEA URCHINS** (Richard Herrmann),
PISASTER STARFISH AND ANEMONES (Richard Herrmann), **CALIFORNIA**
THE INTERTIDAL ZONE, WHERE THESE CREATURES ARE FOUND, IS THE PART OF
THE SHORE THAT IS UNDER WATER AT HIGH TIDE AND EXPOSED WHEN THE TIDE
IS LOW; IT OFTEN SUPPORTS HIGHLY SPECIALIZED COMMUNITIES OF PLANTS AND
ANIMALS, GEARED TO ENDURE THE HARSH CONDITIONS BROUGHT ABOUT BY
WIND AND WAVE.

178   **GIANT STARFISH FEEDING ON MUSSELS, INTERTIDAL ZONE, CALIFORNIA**
(Richard Herrmann)
USING ITS STICKY TUBE FEET, THE CARNIVOROUS STARFISH PRISES OPEN THE
SHELLS OF PREY SUCH AS MUSSELS. STARFISH HAVE NO TEETH. SOME ENGULF
THEIR FOOD, WHILE OTHERS EVERT THEIR STOMACHS ON TO A MEAL: THEY
SECRETE DIGESTIVE ENZYMES OVER THE PREY, WHICH THEY THEN SUCK BACK
INTO THEIR BODIES ALONG WITH THEIR STOMACHS.

179

180

181

179 and 180 **BLADDER-WRACK** (Mark Mattock/Planet Earth),
AND CHANNEL-WRACK (Laurie Campbell), **BRITAIN**
FOUND IN THE MID-SHORE REGION OF ROCKY COASTLINES, AT LOW TIDE THESE
FLATTENED, FORKING SEAWEEDS PROVIDE SHELTER UNDER THEIR DAMP
BLANKET FOR ANIMALS SUCH AS WINKLES AND ANEMONES.

181 **KELP, ORKNEYS, SCOTLAND**
(Mark Mattock/Planet Earth)
BESIDES FURNISHING A HABITAT FOR MARINE CREATURES, MANY KELPS HAVE
LONG BEEN OF COMMERCIAL INTEREST. THE OLD KELP-BURNING INDUSTRY USED
CERTAIN SPECIES IN THE PRODUCTION OF SODA, POTASH AND IODINE, AND SOME
ARE USED NOW AS A SOURCE OF ALGINIC ACID, WHICH IS IMPORTANT AS AN
EMULSIFYING AGENT.

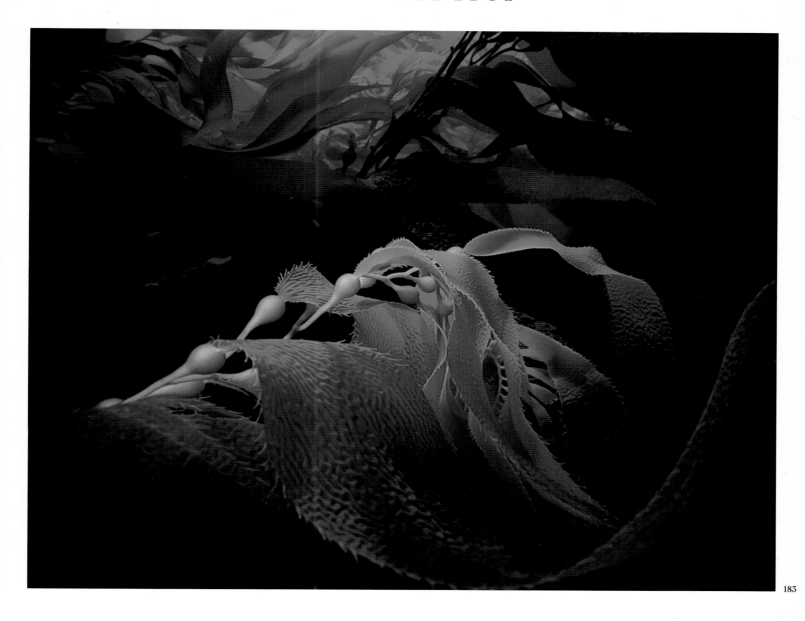

183

182 and 183   A KELP HOLDFAST, IRELAND (John Lythgoe/Planet Earth),
AND A GIANT KELP BLADE, CALIFORNIA (Georgette Douwma/Planet Earth)
THESE LARGE SEAWEEDS OFTEN GROW EXTENSIVELY IN TEMPERATE COASTAL
WATERS, SOMETIMES RESEMBLING ELABORATELY BRANCHED MATS OR LACY
FANS. KELPS HAVE NO ROOTS, BUT ANCHOR THEMSELVES TO THE SEA FLOOR
WITH 'HOLDFASTS', WHICH HELP THEM TO ENDURE ROUGH SEAS. *MACROCYSTIS
PYRIFERA*, THE LARGEST OF THE GIANT KELPS, HAS AT THE BASE OF EACH LEAF-
LIKE BLADE AN AIR BLADDER WHICH MAKES IT BUOYANT IN THE WATER.
SUPPORTED BY THE BLADDERS, THE BLADES FLOAT ON THE WATER'S SURFACE; A
SINGLE FROND MAY BE 60 METRES (200 FT) LONG.

184

184   A SOUTHERN BULL ELEPHANT SEAL, SOUTH ISLAND, NEW ZEALAND

(Donna Kelly)

THE LARGEST OF THE PINNIPEDS, MALE ELEPHANT SEALS OFTEN REACH A
LENGTH OF 5.5 METRES (18 FT) AND WEIGH 2,300 KG (5,000 LB). THEY ARE SOME OF
THE MANY ANIMALS THAT OCCASIONALLY USE FISH-RICH KELP FORESTS AS
HUNTING GROUNDS. ELEPHANT SEALS ARE TRUE SEALS, CLASSED AS SUCH
BECAUSE, UNLIKE FUR SEALS AND SEA LIONS, THEY POSSESS A THICK LAYER OF
BLUBBER AND ARE PROPELLED MAINLY BY THEIR HIND FLIPPERS. THEIR USUALLY
FLOPPY SNOUTS – WHICH GIVE THEM THEIR NAME – FILL WITH AIR WHEN THEY
ARE EXCITED OR ANGRY, PRODUCING A DEEP ROAR WHEN THE AIR IS RELEASED.
DURING THE MATING SEASON THE MALES FIGHT PROLONGED AND BLOODY
BATTLES WITH EACH OTHER. ELEPHANT SEALS USUALLY SLEEP ON THE SHORE
DURING THE DAY, AND FEED AT NIGHT. THE SOUTHERN SPECIES CAN BE FOUND
IN ALL PARTS OF THE WORLD, BUT IS PARTICULARLY WIDESPREAD ON SUB-
ANTARCTIC ISLANDS.

185

185   A GREY WHALE IN A KELP FOREST, OFF THE COAST OF CALIFORNIA
(Howard Hall/Planet Earth)
GREY WHALES MAKE THE LONGEST KNOWN ANNUAL MIGRATION OF ANY
MAMMAL, JOURNEYING UP TO 11,000 KM (7,000 MILES) FROM THEIR SUMMER
FEEDING GROUNDS IN THE ARCTIC AND ANTARCTIC, TO WINTER IN THE BAYS AND
LAGOONS OF TROPICAL COASTAL WATERS, WHERE THEY BREED AND RAISE THEIR
CALVES. THOUGH THEY LIVE MAINLY OFF THEIR BLUBBER DURING THE LONG
MONTHS OF MIGRATION AND BREEDING, THEY WILL OCCASIONALLY BROWSE
AMONG THE KELP FORESTS NEAR THEIR CALVING BAYS; THEY DO NOT EAT THE
SEAWEED ITSELF, BUT INSTEAD GRAZE ON THE THOUSANDS OF MICRO-
ORGANISMS WHICH INHABIT THE KELP BLADES. GREY WHALES ALSO EAT
AMPHIPOD SHRIMPS, WHICH THEY FIND NEAR OR ON THE SEA FLOOR. THEY
APPEAR TO USE THEIR SNOUTS TO STIR UP THE SEDIMENT, AND THEN FILTER THE
DISTURBED ORGANISM-RICH WATER.

186

186 and 187 DAMSELFISH OVER TABLE CORAL, FIJI (B. Jones & M. Shimlock),
AND LION-FISH, SOLOMON ISLANDS (B. Jones & M. Shimlock)
THE SPECTACULAR LIFE OF THE CORAL REEFS: USUALLY OCCURRING IN
LARGE GROUPS ABOVE CORAL HEADS, DAMSELFISH MAINLY EAT PLANKTON,
BUT OCCASIONALLY THEY FEED ON THE ALGAE THAT GROW ON THE CORAL,
INTO WHICH THEY RETREAT AT THE FIRST SIGN OF DANGER. THEY NEVER
STRAY FAR FROM THEIR CHOSEN HOME, IN THIS CASE AN *ACROPORA* CORAL.
THE LION-FISH SHOWN HERE LIVE IN THE HOLES AT THE BASE OF THE RED
SEA-FAN. LIKE ALL OF THE SCORPION-FISH FAMILY, OF WHICH THE LION-
FISH IS A MEMBER, IT HAS VENOMOUS SPINES. DURING THE DAY IT MAY
HIDE IN REEF CREVICES, BECOMING ACTIVE AT NIGHT.

189

189 A YELLOW-CROWNED NIGHT HERON PREENING IN A MANGROVE, SANIBEL ISLAND, FLORIDA
(J. Brian Alker/Planet Earth)
MANY BIRDS ROOST IN MANGROVES, SUCH AS EGRETS AND THE MAINLY NOCTURNAL YELLOW-CROWNED NIGHT HERON. THE MANGROVE SWAMPS OFFER A RICH HUNTING GROUND FOR THE FISH AND CRUSTACEANS ON WHICH THE BIRDS FEED.

188 MANGROVES, BELIZE
(Jim Clare/Partridge Films/OSF)
MANGROVES ARE COASTAL FORESTS THAT GROW IN SALT MARSHES AND TIDAL ESTUARIES, INUNDATED WITH FRESH OR SALT WATER, DEPENDING ON THE TIDE. THE TREES ARE CHARACTERIZED BY WOODY TANGLES OF ROOTS, WHICH MAY BE SUBMERGED FOR LONG INTERVALS; THESE PRODUCE OFFSHOOTS PROJECTING SEVERAL FEET AWAY FROM THE PARENT, WHICH CREATE NEW TREES. SEDIMENT ACCUMULATES UNDER THE MANGROVES' ROOTS.

190

190 MUDSKIPPERS IN A MANGROVE, SOUTH EAST ASIA
(Zig Leszczynski/OSF)
MANGROVE SPECIALISTS, THESE SMALL PREDATORS – ONLY ABOUT 8 CM (3 IN) LONG – ARE EXTREMELY AGGRESSIVE WHEN PURSUING PREY, WHICH INCLUDES SPIDERS, INSECTS, WORMS AND MOLLUSCS. THE PROTRUDING EYE PROVIDES A WIDE-ANGLE VIEW WHEN THE MUDSKIPPER IS SUBMERGED UNDER WATER OR SUNK IN MUD.

CHAPTER TEN

THE HUMAN OCEANS:
PROTECTORS AND PLUNDERERS
Professor Alastair Couper

As far back as we can look in the history of human settlement, people have lived close to the sea, and gathered food and other vital resources from its waters. Certainly, prehistoric peoples were gathering fish, crustaceans and molluscs from around the Great Barrier Reef and Papua New Guinea by 25,000 BC. Others ventured very early across the oceans in search of new homelands; well before 1,500 BC, whole communities pushed out from the island region of southeast Asia into the Pacific.

Thousands of years before it was 'discovered' by Westerners, Polynesian seafarers explored the entire Pacific Ocean – easily the largest feature on the planet, covering one third of its surface – and colonized its many islands. These societies had no mechanical timepieces nor metal tools, but they built fine ships, and possessed a sophisticated understanding of ocean navigation and marine ecology: the knowledge of a culture shaped by the sea.

On the coasts, atolls and islands of the world there are still a few communities who depend on the ocean for survival, people who understand its rhythms and ecology on far more levels than do many modern scientists. On the tiny coral islets of Faraulek, Ifalik and others outlying the Yap island system in Micronesia, people live much as they have done for centuries, benefiting from a treasury of traditional knowledge accumulated over many generations.

So various and complex are the ecosystems of coral reefs that they are still mysterious to most professionals, yet the Yap islanders are accomplished reef ecologists, who exploit their knowledge in precise and sometimes unexpected ways. Travelling the reef flats in small wooden outrigger canoes, they trail

191 A BOY WITH A SHELL, IFALIK, YAP ISLANDS, MICRONESIA
(B. & C. Alexander)
FROM THE EARLIEST TIMES, PEOPLE HAVE LIVED CLOSE TO THE SEA AND HARVESTED FOOD FROM ITS WATERS. BUT, UNDERSTANDING THEIR DEPENDENCE ON THE ENVIRONMENT, THEY HAVE ALSO BEEN CAREFUL TO CONSERVE IT.

baited lines, or dive down with bamboo harpoons to hunt among the coral for lobsters, giant clams, octopus, sea urchins, parrotfish, surgeonfish, goatfish and snappers, and many less familiar animals – some still unnamed by science. Besides food, this bounty is used to make ornaments and tools, while medicines and fishing poisons are manufactured from the very toxins that many reef creatures produce for defence.

Further out at sea in their sailing canoes, Pacific islanders catch large fish such as yellowfin tuna and deep-sea grouper, and even trap dolphins and sharks. Skilled boat-builders and voyagers, they are able to navigate open ocean using only the sun, the waves and stars as guides. Equally subtle signs assist their hunting: schooling animals are located by the behaviour of birds, or the murmur of fish beneath the water; accurate predictions are made according to the phases of the moon, wind direction, currents, and the mood of the sea itself.

Half-way across the world, along the icy sea margins of northwest Greenland and Canada's North West Territories, there are Inuit groups who still live much of the year as hunter gatherers. Large mammals proliferate here, and besides fish the people hunt narwhal and beluga whales, polar bear, walrus, fox and caribou; but the staple diet of coastal Inuit is seal, especially ringed seal – the commonest Arctic species.

Hunting techniques vary with the seasons. During the short polar summer when the sea ice thaws, some hunt whales with harpoons from kayaks. When the sea has frozen over again, they may travel enormous distances by dog sled, or more latterly snowmobile, in search of game. Even otherwise sedentary Inuit make brief expeditions, but some families spend weeks, even months, travelling the ice, occasionally building as they go the temporary shelters which Westerners know as igloos. With a frugality typical of a subsistence lifestyle, the Inuit waste nothing of a kill: excess meat is instantly frozen, or dried; seal fat, a vital source of vitamins and energy, may be stored; sinews become twine and skins become furs, essential protection against the bitter Arctic weather.

But the relationship which the Pacific Islanders, the Inuit and others have with their environment does more than merely inform their hunting techniques. Because they understand the marine ecosystem, they also perceive its vulnerability. Since they are aware that their own survival, and that of future generations, depend upon the welfare of the sea and its inhabitants, they are careful to use its resources in a sustainable, non-destructive way.

In the Pacific Islands, for example, people grasped very early that reef and lagoon resources were finite. Before Samoa fell foul of colonization and industrialization, a complex system of traditional rights, with reef ownership vested from generation to generation in the village chiefs, worked to ensure that the reefs were protected. A similar system is used by indigenous cultures throughout the Coral Islands, Papua New Guinea and elsewhere. In fact, many societies have adopted the strategy of allocating certain stretches of water to particular communities: individuals with a responsibility to their own close-knit group have strong incentives not to over-fish.

Other rules are more specific. In parts of Fiji it is forbidden to take small fish, on the grounds that these are the food of larger fish. Many societies protect certain species during their vulnerable periods – for instance, by closing hunting during spawning time. In the East Sepik region of Papua New Guinea, turtles may not be eaten during certain seasons; elsewhere, dugongs can be consumed only on festive occasions.

Such practices are reinforced by something deeper than economics. They have at their root a reverence for nature which is inherent in traditional societies the world over. In West Africa, shrines are dedicated to sea gods; in Papua New Guinea, complex propitiation rituals take place after a shark capture. The Yap islanders celebrate a dolphin catch with a ceremony of dancing and singing, while the Inuit maintain that every living organism possesses a spirit, which will yield itself willingly to the hunter if treated with proper respect. This means, among other things, no indulging in mass slaughter, even if the animals are many – even when the hunter has a gun, as many Inuit now do. Old taboos have it that only five foxes may be taken on any one hunt. And if too many seals are killed in one place, they will return as humans in boats of ice to take revenge.

Thus rules, values and beliefs forbid over-exploitation, an ethic that has enabled ocean peoples to make a living from the sea for thousands of years. But today, guns have become widespread and missionaries still discourage as pagan a spiritual respect for nature. Many indigenous groups are losing their knowledge and abandoning sustainable hunting practices; settlers are introducing alien values and economies in their place, assaulting traditional cultures at every level. But the greatest threat to the ocean peoples' way of life is the destruction of the marine environment itself.

The logic of protecting the habitat and animals on which you depend seems simple, but it has eluded many more technically advanced cultures, who over the last few hundred years have tended to regard the sea as a free-for-all hunting ground. Indeed the idea of renewable resources is foreign to industrial and high-technology societies that depend on innovation.

Today, the consequences are painfully clear. Creatures such as the great auk and Stellar's sea cow are extinct. Numerous species of fur seal, sea otter, dolphin, great whale, turtle and dugong are endangered, while stocks of many commercial fish – for instance, the bluefin tuna and Newfoundland cod – have fallen to dangerously low levels. Meanwhile, sewage, industrial and radioactive wastes spilling from the coast, or dumped at sea by accident or design, have poisoned the waters of many areas.

There are currently few conservational rules being implemented governing the use of the sea – whether for transport, tourism, waste disposal, energy production, mineral extraction, or commercial fishing – though all these can, and frequently do, damage marine ecosystems. Since 1982, countries have had sovereignty over 320-km (200-mile) Exclusive Economic Zones extending from their coasts, but most have not yet begun to use sustainably the resources within them. This bodes ill for the future, especially now that new mineral, oil and natural gas resources have been discovered beneath the sea, and technological advances may soon enable them to be extracted.

Growing populations will put further pressure on the over-stretched oceans. Already, 70 per cent of people live on or near the coasts. Given that within sixty or seventy years, world populations are likely to rise from the current five billion to around twelve billion, the demands made on the sea will be greater than ever before.

If we are to meet the complex challenges of the future, long-term planning must replace short-sighted exploitation; technological progress must be combined with sustainable use of the sea's resources. Approaches could include marine agriculture, energy production, even mining; much is possible, providing the limitations of the environment and balance of the ecosystem are taken into account.

In a gradual move towards protecting and conserving the whole marine environment as distinct from individual species, some countries are introducing measures such as fishing-gear restrictions, prohibited fishing areas, and closed seasons during spawning. Such practices are familiar to ocean peoples. Indeed, it has been argued that all the conservation methods which Western societies are only now considering have been employed by island societies for centuries.

We can no longer afford to underestimate the knowledge and understanding of ocean peoples. Neither should we continue to undervalue the importance of their deep-held respect for the oceans, which contrasts sharply with the 'land-mindedness' even of governments whose countries are surrounded by sea. Consider the Indonesian word *tanahair*, which translates as 'homeland', but literally means 'homelandwater'. Here lies the crux. The people of the oceans do not regard land as the centre of the universe, the seas merely as a convenient dumping ground and resource to be plundered. They know that both are necessary parts of a greater whole.

---

192 A REEF FISHERMAN WITH HIS CATCH, YAP, MICRONESIA
(B. & C. Alexander)
FISHERMEN OF THE CORAL ISLANDS OF YAP DIVE FOR FISH ON THE REEFS BY NIGHT, EQUIPPED WITH JUST A SPEAR, A TORCH AND A MASK. THE FISH ARE ATTRACTED BY THE LIGHT, AND HAULS ARE OFTEN RICH. LOCAL MARTIN LUGWAN DISPLAYS HIS NIGHT'S CATCH OF LOBSTER AND FISH.

194

193   LABUAN HADJI VILLAGE, BORNEO
(B. Jones and M. Shimlock)

MUCH OF THE COASTAL FRINGE OF BORNEO IS LOW-LYING AND SWAMPY. LABUAN HADJI IS ONE OF THE OLDEST 'WATER VILLAGES' IN THE AREA; MOST CHILDREN LEARN TO SWIM AND PADDLE A CANOE BEFORE THEY CAN WALK. THE PEOPLE HAVE A LONG TRADITION OF LIVING VERY CLOSE TO THE SEA. NEARLY EVERYONE MAKES THEIR LIVELIHOOD FROM IT, AND MOST STILL USE TRADITIONAL SAILING CRAFT TO FISH FROM. MANY HOUSES HAVE NETS SLUNG BETWEEN THEM FOR TRAPPING BAIT, WHICH IS LATER USED FOR FISHING.

194   A FISHING AND BOAT-BUILDING VILLAGE, BONE RATE, INDONESIA
(David Hall)

IN THIS SMALL VILLAGE IN THE BONE RATE GROUP OF ISLANDS IN CENTRAL INDONESIA, THE MAIN LIVELIHOODS ARE BOAT-BUILDING AND FISHING. AS WELL AS BEING FISHING VESSELS, THE BOATS ARE USED FOR TRANSPORT BETWEEN ISLANDS. THE COUNTRY CONSISTS OF 13,677 ISLANDS, STRETCHING IN A CRESCENT FOR MORE THAN 5,000 KM (3,200 MILES), FROM THE INDIAN OCEAN TO THE PACIFIC. SIX THOUSAND OF THE ISLANDS ARE INHABITED; IN 1890 FOSSILS OF JAVA MAN (*HOMO ERECTUS*) WERE FOUND HERE, DATING BACK 500,000 YEARS.

195

195 and 196   CHINESE FISHING NETS AT COCHIN, ON THE ARABIAN SEA, INDIA
(Colin Caket/Zefa), AND MOZAMBIQUAN FISHERMEN
DRAGGING IN THEIR CATCH (V. Wentzel/Zefa)
AMONG BOTH TRADITIONAL AND INDUSTRIALIZED FISHERMEN, NETS STILL
CONSTITUTE, ALL OVER THE WORLD, THE MOST POPULAR MEANS OF GATHERING
THE SEAS' HARVEST. CANTILEVER FISHING NETS (195) ARE AN ANCIENT IMPORT
FROM CHINA. THE FISHERMEN SHOWN OPPOSITE, ON THE COAST OF
MOZAMBIQUE NEAR WHERE THE ZAMBEZI RIVER FLOWS INTO THE INDIAN
OCEAN, ARE HAULING IN THEIR CATCH IN A NET SET SOME TIME PREVIOUSLY.

197   STILT FISHING, GALLE, SRI LANKA
(Heather Angel)
STILT FISHING IS ANOTHER ANCIENT AND EXTREMELY SIMPLE BUT EFFICIENT
TECHNIQUE USED BY MANY COASTAL COMMUNITIES. THE STILTS ARE PLACED AT
FIXED SITES, ALLOWING FISHING IN DEEPER WATER, WHERE FISH ARE OFTEN
LARGER AND MORE PLENTIFUL.

196

197

198   DRYING A SQUID, MADAGASCAR
(Frans Lanting/Zefa)

IN HOT REGIONS, DRYING IS THE STANDARD WAY OF PRESERVING FISH,
THOUGH IT IS OFTEN ALSO SALTED. THROUGH MUCH OF SOUTH EAST ASIA,
EAST AFRICA AND THE MEDITERRANEAN, SQUID HAS LONG BEEN A STAPLE;
IT IS ONLY RECENTLY THAT IT HAS BECOME A COMMERCIAL SPECIES IN THE
USA AND OTHER PARTS OF EUROPE. THIS VEZO FISHERMAN, BELONGING TO
A FISHING COMMUNITY IN THE SOUTH OF MADAGASCAR, USES TIME-
HONOURED METHODS TO MAKE HIS LIVELIHOOD; HIS MOST ESSENTIAL
ASSET IS HIS OUTRIGGER CANOE. FISHING IN MADAGASCAR TAKES PLACE
LARGELY IN COASTAL LAGOONS.

199

199, 200 and 201   MUSSEL-HARVESTING AT SCARDOVARI, ITALY (Zefa),
A SOUTH EAST ASIAN FISHERMAN (Holdsworth/Zefa) **AND AN INUIT FISHERMAN
WITH A HARPOON, GREENLAND** (B. & C. Alexander)
SMALL POPULATIONS AND NON-MECHANIZED TECHNOLOGY, COMBINED WITH A
KNOWLEDGE OF THE SEA AND RESPECT FOR ITS LIFE, HAVE ALLOWED COASTAL
PEOPLES TO HARVEST THE SEA'S BOUNTY FOR CENTURIES, WHILE DAMAGING IT
NOT IN THE SLIGHTEST. OFTEN THEIR FISHING METHODS ARE SELECTIVE, SO
THAT THE MINIMUM NUMBER OF FISH ARE TAKEN – IN SHARP CONTRAST TO THE
SWEEP NETS AND HUGE TRAWLERS USED BY THE COMMERCIAL FISHING
INDUSTRY, WHICH 'VACUUM' ALL THE LIFE FROM WHATEVER STRETCH OF SEA
THEY TARGET.

200

201

202   FISHING CANOES OFF THE EAST COAST OF SRI LANKA
(Starfoto/Zefa)
MANY COASTAL PEOPLES ARE EXTREMELY ACCOMPLISHED BOAT-BUILDERS AND
NAVIGATORS, DESPITE HAVING NO INDUSTRIAL TECHNOLOGY, AND MANY STILL
USE TRADITIONAL CRAFT MADE SOLELY FROM NATURAL MATERIALS. FOR PEOPLE
WHO SUBSIST FROM THE SEA, A FISHING BOAT IS A FAMILY'S MOST ESSENTIAL
POSSESSION.

203

203   FISHING BOATS AT ERQUY, BRITTANY, FRANCE

(B. & C. Alexander)

EVEN IN EUROPE THERE ARE STILL TRADITIONAL FISHING COMMUNITIES WHOSE SMALL-SCALE OPERATIONS PROVIDE A LIVELIHOOD FOR THE VILLAGE YET ARE SUSTAINABLE WITHOUT HARMING THE ENVIRONMENT. HERE, FISHERMEN APPROACH THE HARBOUR AFTER A DAY'S FISHING. KEEPING BOTH BOATS AND NETS IN GOOD REPAIR IS A HABITUAL TASK.

204   COD-FISHING, NEWFOUNDLAND

(B. & C. Alexander)

EACH SUMMER, THE SMALL CAPELIN FISH HURL THEMSELVES ON TO THE GRAVEL SHORE TO SPAWN, WHEREUPON THEY ARE PURSUED BY SCHOOLS OF COD. THESE FISHERMEN LAY OUT THEIR NETS CLOSE TO THE SHORELINE, IN SUCH A WAY THAT THE COD ARE CHANNELLED INTO A LARGE NET BOX, WHICH THEY EMPTY DAILY. HERE THE CREW ARE HAULING IN THE COD TRAP. SUCH SMALL-SCALE FISHING IS UNLIKELY TO AFFECT COD STOCKS, BUT FISH FACTORY VESSELS HAVE GREATLY DEPLETED THE POPULATIONS OF THIS COMMERCIALLY IMPORTANT FISH – POSSIBLY PERMANENTLY.

204

205

205 ISLANDERS PREPARE TO DISEMBARK, SATAWAL, MICRONESIA
(B. & C. Alexander)
ISOLATED FROM THE REST OF THE YAP ISLANDS, SATAWAL IS DEPENDENT
ON THIS CARGO AND PASSENGER BOAT TO BRING SUPPLIES AND A DOCTOR
EVERY FEW MONTHS, AND TO TRANSPORT LOCAL PRODUCTS FOR SALE
ELSEWHERE.

206 A FLOATING FISH STALL, THAILAND
(Robert Harding Picture Library)
FLOATING MARKET STALLS SELLING FISH AND OTHER PRODUCE ARE A
COMMON SIGHT AROUND THAILAND'S MANY SMALL ISLANDS. BOTH MARINE
AND FRESHWATER FISHING ARE IMPORTANT TO THE THAI ECONOMY.
MACKEREL, SHARK, SHRIMPS AND CRABS ARE EXPORTED, AND FISH STILL
PROVIDES MOST OF THE PROTEIN IN THE PEOPLE'S DIET. BUT THE SHALLOW
COASTAL WATERS OF THE GULF OF THAILAND ARE BEING GROSSLY OVER-
FISHED BY COMMERCIAL INTERESTS.

209

207 and 208   AN INUK WITH HIS DOG TEAM (B. & C. Alexander), **AND AN INUK JIGGING FOR POLAR COD** (B. & C. Alexander), **CANADA**

ONCE THE SEA HAS FROZEN OVER AT THE BEGINNING OF THE WINTER, THE INUIT FIND THEIR HUNTING GROUNDS GREATLY EXTENDED. POLAR BEAR HUNTS, INVOLVING JOURNEYS OVER SEA ICE, USING SLEDS DRAWN BY DOG TEAMS, CAN LAST FOR FOUR TO SIX WEEKS. IN SPRING THE SEA ICE BEGINS TO MELT, AND HUNTING ON IT BECOMES DANGEROUS. FISHING THROUGH HOLES IN THE ICE IS AN EASY, IF TEDIOUS, ALTERNATIVE. ONCE CAUGHT, THE FISH WILL FREEZE ALMOST INSTANTLY IN THE AIR – WHEN THIS PHOTOGRAPH (208) WAS TAKEN THE TEMPERATURE WAS −35° CENTIGRADE.

210

209 and 210   AN INUK PREPARING A SEAL NET (B. & C. Alexander), **AND AN IGLOO AT NIGHT** (B. & C. Alexander), **NORTHWEST GREENLAND**

BEFORE THE SEA FULLY FREEZES IN OCTOBER, THE INUIT TRAVEL TO PLACES WHERE THE SEALS ARE MANY. NETS ARE STRUNG OUT BETWEEN TWO HOLES IN THE ICE BELOW THE SURFACE, AND WEIGHTED DOWN WITH STONES WHERE THE CURRENT IS STRONG; SEALS ARE SWEPT INTO THE CURTAIN OF NET AND HAULED UP. ON LONG HUNTING TRIPS SOME INUIT STILL BUILD THE SHELTERS THAT WE KNOW AS IGLOOS; ONE PERSON CAN CONSTRUCT AN IGLOO IN ABOUT AN HOUR. INUIT HAVE NEVER USED THEM AS PERMANENT HOMES.

CONCLUSION

ROGER HAMMOND

ROCKS MIRROR THE RAVAGES OF WEATHER OVER CENTURIES, AND PEOPLE'S faces hold a lifetime's experience. The sea does not record the passage of time on its endlessly shifting surface: it is almost impossible to comprehend that over three and a half thousand million years have passed since the oceans spawned the first, primitive living organisms.

Evolution works on a giant time scale which defies the imagination. Consider, for example, that small, hooved, dog-like creatures inhabiting prehistoric beaches were the ancestors of today's great whales. The extraordinary metamorphosis took place as generation after generation was selected and refined over some fifty million years. This enormous length of time is nonetheless just a moment in the history of the oceans, and in the history of life itself.

In evolutionary terms, human beings appeared on the scene very recently indeed. They quickly developed a relationship with the sea; communities were living and fishing along the oceans' margins well before 25,000 BC, and by 3,000 BC many were accomplished seafarers. People have exploited the oceans for transport, food and other resources ever since. But until just two or three hundred years ago, we had little impact on the ecosystem: the sea retained ultimate control. Storms wrecked thousand upon thousand of vessels, taking crews and cargo to the ocean bed. Their remains were rapidly assimilated, and the sea's ancient life processes continued, undisturbed.

We are probably little different from our ancestors, but the world we inhabit is dramatically changed. In less than a century, the global population has exploded from 1,700 million to nearly 5,000 million. And thanks to the Industrial Revolution, we have at our disposal powers that our forebears could not have dreamed of. Such conditions have brought unprecedented pressures to bear on the oceans – this most vital of the planet's life support systems.

In the briefest moment of evolutionary time, we have reversed our relationship with the sea: today, we are the ones in control. It is a power we greatly abuse. We are decimating fish stocks and endangering other creatures with indiscriminate fishing methods. Miles of drift-nets spare none; huge factory ships remove hundreds of tonnes of marine life in a single catch. But perhaps even more destructive than this constant depleting is what we pour into the sea. Toxic materials from factories, power stations, ocean tankers, sewage plants and agricultural land are discharged or deliberately dumped into the water. Animals are poisoned and entire species threatened by these alien substances. The thinning ozone layer may present an even graver long-term danger, for it appears to be affecting the growth of phytoplankton – the base of the entire marine ecosystem.

There is one power that we have greatly under-used. We possess at least some understanding of the oceans' global importance, and also of our own impact on them. To date, we have concentrated solely on developing new ways of exploiting more of the sea's resources. We must now begin to channel our abilities differently, and discover how we may balance our needs with what the oceans can provide. The changed world demands a change in attitudes and practices: we must respond to this challenge, if we are to safeguard both our own future, and the oceans'.

A NORTH SEA OIL RIG IN ROUGH WEATHER

(Arnulf Husmo/Tony Stone Worldwide)

ONLY IN THE LAST TWO HUNDRED AND FIFTY YEARS OR SO HAVE HUMAN BEINGS BEEN ABLE TO HARNESS THE SEA'S POWER AND MINERAL RESOURCES, BUT IN THAT TIME WE HAVE DONE IMMEASURABLE DAMAGE TO THE MARINE ECOSYSTEM. CAN WE NOW LEARN TO USE THE OCEANS IN A LESS DESTRUCTIVE WAY?

THE LIVING EARTH FOUNDATION

LIVING EARTH IS ONE OF A NUMBER OF ORGANIZATIONS working internationally to help bring about change. The human being has the unique quality of being able to look forward in time. Our governments must learn to be responsible for the future, just as individuals must learn to be responsible to future generations.

As individuals, at a national level, use your voting and lobbying rights to ensure that politicians develop new regional and international agreements to protect marine ecosystems. At a regional level, ensure that marine parks and protected coastlands are established. By exercising your discretion as a consumer, exert a direct impact on corporations that exploit the oceans. As we approach the end of the twentieth century, it is up to us all to ensure that we can celebrate the oceans' next millennium as well as the present one.

By buying this book you are helping to fund our work along coastal areas in Cameroon, Brazil and Venezuela. Fragile ecosystems in these countries are increasingly under threat of over-exploitation, but by involving local people in conservation and management, Living Earth is turning the tide. Its environmental education programmes are empowering local communities to understand and value their natural heritage and initiate changes in the way they use natural resources.

If you wish to know more about the work of Living Earth, further information can be obtained from our UK office.

Living Earth Foundation,
The Old Laundry, Ossington Buildings,
Moxon Street, London W1M 3JD

CONTRIBUTORS

PROFESSOR DAVID BELLAMY, botanist, writer and broadcaster, is co-founder of the Conservation Foundation and Vice-President of the Marine Conservation Society.

DR JULIAN CALDECOTT is an ecologist. As Biodiversity Management Adviser to the Indonesian government, he has worked on policy issues concerning many large coastal and marine reserves.

DR TUNDI AGARDY is Marine Conservation Scientist for the World Wildlife Fund in the USA.

DR IAN JOINT is a Project Leader at the Plymouth Marine Laboratory of the Natural Environment Research Council, and has worked on various aspects of phytoplankton ecology for the past twenty years.

MARK SIMMONDS is a campaigning marine biologist and Senior Lecturer in Environmental Sciences at the University of Greenwich in London. He has worked closely for several years with Greenpeace, focusing on the impacts of pollution on marine wildlife.

DR MARTIN ANGEL is head of the Biology Department at the Institute of Oceanographic Sciences, Deacon Laboratory, Surrey. In addition to his chapter, he has provided a great deal of expertise and support in the preparation of this book.

DR PETER HERRING is Senior Scientist in the Biology Department of the Institute of Oceanographic Sciences, Deacon Laboratory, Surrey.

DR ANDREW WATSON is Senior Scientist at the Plymouth Marine Laboratory.

SIR ANTHONY LAUGHTON is a marine geophysicist who has researched into the nature and origin of the geology of the ocean basins. His special interest is the shape and structure of the ocean floor. He is the former Director of the Institute of Oceanographic Sciences, Surrey, and a past President of the Challenger Society for Marine Science.

DR NICHOLAS POLUNIN is a Lecturer in the Department of Marine Sciences and Coastal Management at the University of Newcastle.

PROFESSOR ALASTAIR COUPER teaches in the Department of Maritime Studies, University of Wales, Cardiff, and is the former Editor of the *Times Atlas of the Oceans*.

ROGER HAMMOND is the Founder Director and Chief Executive of Living Earth.

LISA SILCOCK is a freelance writer, photographer and film-maker with a special interest in environmental issues. She was assistant producer of Channel 4's award-winning series, *Baka – People of the Rainforest*. She edited the previous book in this series, *The Rainforests: A Celebration*, and has contributed to numerous national publications.

HELEN GILKS, who researched the illustrations for this book, manages the international Wildlife Photographer of the Year Competition.

DAMIEN LEWIS is an award-winning journalist and film-maker, who specializes in environment and development issues.

ROBERT BISSET is a Director of the World Press Centre, and the co-ordinator of their Oceans Service.

ACKNOWLEDGEMENTS

The publishers would like to thank the following individuals and agencies for permission to use their photographs in this book:

BRYAN & CHERRY ALEXANDER
Higher Cottage
Manston
Sturminster Newton
Dorset DT10 1EZ
UK
tel 0258 473006

HEATHER ANGEL/BIOFOTOS
Highways
6 Vicarage Hill
Farnham
Surrey GU9 8HJ
UK
tel 0252 716700

LAURIE CAMPBELL
Rosewell Cottage
Paxton
Berwick-upon-Tweed TD15 1TE
tel 0289 86736

GERRY ELLIS NATURE
PHOTOGRAPHY
6208 South West 32nd Avenue
Portland
Oregon 97201
USA
fax 503 452 1914

DAVID HALL
257 Ohayo Mountain Road
Woodstock
New York 12498
USA
fax 914 334 4788

ROBERT HARDING PICTURE
LIBRARY
58-59 Great Marlborough Street
London W1V 1DD
tel 071 287 5414

RICHARD HERRMANN
12545 Mustang Drive
Poway
CA 92064
USA
tel 619 679 7017

INSTITUTE OF OCEANOGRAPHIC
SCIENCES (IOS)
Wormley
Godalming
Surrey GU9 5UB
UK
tel 0428 684141

BURT JONES & MAURINE
SHIMLOCK
Secret Sea Visions
PO Box 162931
Austin
Tex. 78716
USA
tel/fax 512 328 1201

J. MICHAEL KELLY
102 East Moore
Suite 245
Terrell
Tex. 75160
USA
fax 214 563 2515

ARMIN MAYWALD
Graf Moltke Strasse 59
2800 Bremen 1
Germany
tel 0421 358 907

MINDEN PICTURES
24 Seascape Village
Aptos
CA 95003
USA
fax 408 685 1911

DAVID NOTON
20 Doone Road
Horfield
Bristol BS7 0JG
UK
tel 0272 512489

BEN OSBORNE
c/o Oxford Scientific Films
Lower Road
Long Hanborough
Oxfordshire OX8 8LL
UK
tel 0993 881881

OXFORD SCIENTIFIC FILMS
(OSF)
Lower Road
Long Hanborough
Oxfordshire OX8 8LL
UK
tel 0993 881881

LINDA PITKIN
12 Coningsby Road
South Croydon
Surrey CR2 6QP
UK

PLANET EARTH PICTURES
4 Harcourt Street
London W1H 1DS
tel 071 262 4427

GRAHAM ROBERTSON
c/o Australian Antarctic Division
Channel Highway
Kingston
Tasmania 7050
Australia

JEFF ROTMAN PHOTOGRAPHY
14 Cottage Avenue
Somerville
MA 02144
USA
fax 617 666 4811

TONY STONE WORLDWIDE
Worldwide House
116 Bayham Street
London NW1 0BA
tel 071 267 7166

KIM WESTERSKOV
20 Greerton Road
Tauranga
New Zealand
tel 75 785 138

NORBERT WU
165 Ivy Drive
Orinda
CA 94563
USA
fax 510 376 8864

ZEFA PICTURE LIBRARY
20 Conduit Place
London W2 1HZ
tel 071 262 0101

Italic page numbers refer to captions

abalone 174
Acropora coral *25*
albacore 36
albatrosses *70*, *174*, *179*; black-browed *77*; migration 80
algae 36, 172, 173, 174, *185*; *see also* phytoplankton, zooxanthellae
ammonia 59
amphipods 65
Amphiprion frenatus 117
anemones 26, 96, *100*, *101*, *102*, *104*, 111, *117*, 173, 174, *185*
angelfish 7, *99*
anglerfish 95, 114, *108*, *109*, *125*
animal phyla 10
Antarctic conditions 59
Antarctic divergence 78
Antarctic icebergs *156*
Arabian Sea 156, *204*
Arctic conditions 59
Arctic terns, 80, *91*
arrow-worms 58, *67*
atmosphere, and the oceans 131–2, *155*
atolls, *166*, *169*

bacteria 130; synthesizers of energy 154; used in light-making 114, *126*
balloonfish, spiny *42*
barnacles: acorn *159*; coastal 174; goose *147*
barracuda 11, *14*
basslets (sea-perch) *12*; fairy *40*
beaches *166*
Bengal, Bay of 156
Bering Sea 78
'biological pump' 131–2
bioluminescence 37, 112–14, *122*, *125*, *126*
biomass *see* photosynthesis
birds 60, *70*; coastal 172; colonies *181*; migration 80
'black smokers' *see* hydrothermal vents
bladder-wrack *187*
bonito 36
Borneo *205*
boxfish, spotted 11
breeding 93, 94–6, 114, 171
bryozoans 10, 174
by-the-wind sailor (*velella*) *45*

cabezon 174
calcium carbonate 131, *159*
camouflage 111, 113, *114*, *121*, *126*
Canada *217*
carbon dioxide 7, 58, 131, 132, *155*
Caribbean 79, 112, 172–3
caribou 198
channel-wrack *187*
chemicals *see* nutrients
chitons 174
chlorophyll *see* photosynthesis
clams: coastal 172, 173; giant 130, *149*, 154
cleaners *see* scavengers; shrimps
cliffs *161*, *165*

climate: effect on the sea 77–8; influence of the oceans on 10, 131–2
clouds 7
clown-fish 96, 111, *117*, 173
coastal environment 171–4; habitats 37, 171
coastline *161*, *162*
coccolithophores (algae) 7
cod 199, *211*, *217*; blue *15*
colour, and marine animals 111–12, 113, *117*
comb-jellies 36, *122*
communication between animals 111–27
concealment *see* camouflage
conservation, rules of 199–200
continental shelves 153, 156
continents, movement 12, 155
copepods 36, 58, 60, *66*, 94
coral: *Acropora 25*; chalice *5*; fire *104*; in food chain 11; horny *17*, *18*; tube *27*; types 173
coral islands *169*
coral lagoons *169*
coral reefs 7, *12*, 38, *40*, *166*, 173, *192*; and humans 197–8; *197*
corallimorph *27*
cowries 173
crabs 11, *66*, 130, 154; coastal 172, 173, 174; fiddler *172*; hermit *104*; sponge *145*
crocodile-fish *121*
crustaceans *66*, 112, 113–14; *see also* larvae
ctenophorans 11

damselfish *192*; *see also* garibaldi
Darwin, Charles, on luminescence 112
decapods 126
Diacria major 60, *106*
diatoms 57, 59–60
dinoflagellates 112
dolphins 79, 198, 199; bottlenose 79, *85*
dugong 199
Durdle Door (Dorset) *155*

earth: crust 154–5; origin of life 129; regulatory system 131–2
earthquakes 155, 156
East Pacific Rise 154
echinoderms *see* brittle-stars; sea cucumbers; sea urchins; starfish
ecosystem, ocean 9–33, 171–95, 219
eels 37; freshwater 79; larvae *66*, 89; wolf *45*
eggs: as food 94; octopus *107*; squid *107*
elements 129–30
energy *see* photosynthesis
environment, sea as 35–8
Ephyrina figueriae 126
estuaries *161*, 172
Eurythenes gryllus 150
evolution of sea creatures 37, 219

Exclusive Economic Zones 200
eyes of marine creatures 112, 113–14, *118*

fan-worms *147*
feeding 93–6
Fiji 199
filefish 11, *21*
filter-feeders 11
firefleas 112, 114
fishing *200*, *204*, *208*, *210*, *211*, *212*, *217*; coastal waters 171, 174
flashlight fish 37, 114, *126*
flats *see* sandflats
flatworm, leopard 11
Florida Bay Keys 172
flounder, peacock *121*
food, search for 93–6
food chain 11, 36, 58
food web 59–60
fossil fuels 132, *156*
foxes 198, 199
France, fishing *211*
frigate birds 172
furbelow 173
fusiliers *2*

gannets *181*
garibaldi *9*, 174
geomorphology, marine 153–6
Giant's Causeway (Co. Antrim) *158*
glaciations 132, *156*
glass-fish, Indian 113
gorgonians (horny corals) *17*, *18*, *21*
grass meadows, underwater 172–3, *185*
great auk 199
Great Barrier Reef *166*, 173
Greenland *156*, *208*, *217*
grey angel fish *7*
groupers: coral *5*, *99*; deep-sea 198; Nassau *47*
Gulf Stream 78, 79
gulls 174
gurnard, flying 111
gyres (circulating water masses) 60, 77–8

habitats 35–8, 171–4; variety 37
hatchet-fish 113, *126*
Hawaii 156, *159*
hawkfish *18*
heart-urchins 11
hermaphroditism in animals 95, *106*, *117*
Hermissenda crassicornis 29
herons 172, *195*
herring 171
Himalayas 155–6
humans: influence on the earth 132; and the oceans 197–217, 219
hunting 197–8; rules 199
hydroids, sea-fan 10
hydrothermal vents 130, 154, *158*

ice ages 132, *156*
icebergs *156*

igloos *217*
Indonesia 12, *203*
Inuit people and the sea 198, 199, *208*, *217*
isopods 36
Italy, mussel-harvesting *208*

jawfish, yellowhead 95
jellyfish 10, 36, 37, *46*, *66*, 113, *122*; coastal 172; lion's mane *49*; luminous *125*; miniature 58

kelp 37, 38, *58*, *141*, 171, 173, *187*, *189*, *191*
Kilauea Rift 156
Kilauea volcano *159*
kittiwakes *181*
krill 59–60, 65, 69, 78, 94

Labuan Hadji *205*
lagoons *169*
landslides, underwater 156
lantern fish 94
larvae, marine 11, 58, *65*, 94, 96; of anglerfish *109*; of eels *66*, 79, 89; as food 94; transparency of some 113, *125*
lava flows, subterranean 154, *156*, *158*
lichens 174
life, origin in the sea 35, 129
light, penetration of sea 36, 37, 112; *see also* bioluminescence, photosynthesis
limpets 174
Linophryne indica 95, *108*
lion-fish *192*
lobster: coastal 173; larvae *125*
Loligo opalescens 107
luminosity *see* bioluminescence
lures 94, 114, *125*

mackerel 36, *58*
Macrocystis pyrifera 171, *189*
Madagascar, fishing *206*
magma 155, *159*
man *see* humans
manatee *54*, 173; *see also* sea cow
mangroves 12, 37, 38, 172, *195*
Marianas Trench 154
'marine deserts' 60
marine environment *see* environment
'marine snow' 131, 154
marlin 36
mating *see* reproduction
microbes 129, 131
Micronesia *197*, *197*, *200*, *212*
Mid-Atlantic Ridge 154
Mid-Indian Ocean Ridge 154
migrations, marine 77–91
minerals: from kelp *187*; in the ocean 130, 131, *141*, *166*
molluscs *152*
moon jellies 36, *125*
moon snails 172
mountains, submarine 154, 155–6
Mozambiquan fishermen *204*

mudflats 172
mudskippers 172, *195*
mullet 172
mussels 174, *185*; harvesting *208*

narwhal 198
nautilus, chambered *105*
needlefish, crocodile 11
Nembrotha cristata 29
Newfoundland *211*
night herons, yellow-crowned *195*
nitrates 58
nudibranchs *see* sea-slugs
nutrients in the sea 36, 58, 59, 172

ocean floor *see* seabed
ocean ridges 154
oceans: ecosystems 9–33; varied
  environments 10–11; function in
  relation to earth 129–30; mass
  35; site of life's origin 35; surface
  area 7, 131
octopus 50, *107*
oil pollution 7, 219
oil rig *219*
ostracods 95–6, *106*, 150
oyster-catcher 172
oysters, coastal 172
ozone layer 219

Pacific butterfly fish *46*
Pacific Ocean, colonization 197, 198,
  199
palola worms 95
Pandalus prawns *145*
Papua New Guinea 198, 199
parrotfish 11, *18*; eyes *118*;
  reproduction 95
pelicans 172
penguins 59–60; Adélie *75*;
  chinstrap *72*, *177*; king *177*
Periclimenes 101, *102*
periwinkle 174
phosphates 58
photic zone 36–7
photosynthesis 11, 57–8, *62*, 155
Physophora hydrostatica 48
phytoplankton 11, 36, 57, *57*, 60, *62*,
  130, 131, *155*; growth of 58, 59,
  78, 219
pinnipeds *see* seals
plaice 111; larvae 113
plankton 57–60; coastal waters 172;
  seabed 154; *see also*
  phytoplankton, zooplankton
plates, tectonic 155, *161*
Point of Stoer (Scotland) *162*

polar bears *74*, *75*, 198
pollution 12, 199, 219; coastal 174;
  coral reefs 38; oil 7
populations, rising 200
Portuguese man-o'-war *45*
prawns: Jordan's *145*; scarlet 94
protection of species 199
protozoa 60
pteropods (*Diacria major*) 60, *106*
pufferfish: eyes *118*; guineafowl *45*;
  starry *25*; *see also* balloonfish
pullers *40*

ray, manta *55*
red Irish lord *22*
reefs *see* coral reefs
reproduction 93, 94–6, *99*, *106*, *107*,
  114
resources, submarine 200
Rhizophora 172
rock, as seabed 11–12
rock pools 174

salmon, migration 79, *89*, 96
salp 95
salt 130
salt marshes 172
sandflats, sediment *159*, *161*
sandpiper 172
Sargasso Sea, and eels 79
sargassum 36, 79
sawfish *52*
scavengers 130–1, *145*, *147*, 150;
  coastal 173
scorpion-fish *121*; spotted 111; *see also*
  lion-fish
sea *see* oceans
sea butterfly 60, *106*
sea cow 173, 199; Stellar's 199; *see
  also* manatee
sea cucumbers 11, *149*, 150
sea-fan *17*
sea floor *see* seabed
sea horse *20*
sea lace 173
sea levels 12
sea lions 80, *85*, 85
sea otters 174, 199
sea-pens 113
sea-perch (basslets) *12*, 40
sea shells 131, *159*
sea-slugs *29*; *Glaucus 45*; *Hermissenda
  crassicornis 29*; lettuce *31*;
  Nembrotha cristata 29; Spanish
  dancer, eggs *30*; Spanish shawl *29*
sea-snails *45*, 173
sea-snake *51*

sea-squirt 174
sea tangle 173
sea turtle 36, 37
sea urchins *55*, 173, 174, *185*; fire *55*;
  radiant star *55*; skeletons *159*;
  slate pencil *55*
sea-water: composition 130; as life
  medium 36
seabed 11–12, 153–6; absorption of
  elements 130; environment 37;
  mobility 154–5
seabirds 80, *165*, 174
seals 68, 77; coastal 174; crab-eater
  68; elephant *85*, *190*; fur *80*, 199;
  grey 79; harp 79, *85*; ringed 198
seaweeds 173, 174; *see also* kelp
sediment: and earthquakes 156;
  eroded *166*; on ocean bed 11, 58,
  142, 156; sandflat *159*
sex *see* reproduction
sex changes 95, *98*
shags, blue-eyed *181*
sharks 198; blue *38*; coastal 172,
  174; hammerhead *55*; mako 36;
  requiem 11; white 174
shearwater *91*
sheepshead 174
shrimps 11, 58, 113, 114, 130;
  anemone *102*; camouflage 113;
  cleaner *100*, *101*, *104*; coastal 172,
  173; opossum 94–5, *104*; Pederson
  cleaner *47*
signalling between animals 111–27
silica 131
silversides *15*
siphonophores 10; *Physophora
  hydrostatica 48*; *see also* Portuguese
  man-o'-war
snails *see* sea-snails
sole, larvae 113
spawning 95, 171
species: fish 38; marine 7, 36
sponges 130, *142*; azure vase *142*;
  coastal 172; encrusting *142*; tube
  129
squid 37, 113; Caribbean reef *51*;
  drying *206*; *Loligo opalescens 107*
Sri Lanka, fishing *204*, *210*
Stair Hole (Dorset) *161*
starfish *55*, 173, 174, *182*; crown-of-
  thorns 11; giant *185*; pisaster *185*
sulphur 154
sunfish 94
sunlight and the sea 36, 58–9; *see
  also* photosynthesis
surf grass *185*
surface water 58, 59

swallower, black *108*

tanabair 200
tarpon *15*, *111*, 172
temperate oceans 59; ecology 174,
  182
temperatures, rising 38
Thailand *212*
Themisto compressa 65
tidal zone 174, *185*
transparency as camouflage 113, *125*
trevallies, big-eye 114
triggerfish, Picasso 11
Troodos Massif (Cyprus) 155
tropic-birds, white-tailed *91*
tropical regions 60, 172; coastal
  environment 172–3
tube-worms 154
tuna 198, 199
turban shell *152*
turbidity currents 156
turtles: green *54*; 79, *89*; laying eggs
  171; loggerhead 79; migration
  79–80, 96; restrictions 199
tuskfish, harlequin *98*

urchins *see* sea urchins

Vargula cypridina 106
velella 45
volcanoes 12, 155, *156*, *159*, *166*

walrus *80*, 198
Warren Point (Devon) *162*
water, as basis of life 7, 130–1
water hopper *65*
waves *155*, *165*
weather and the sea 10, 77–8, 131–2
weeds, surface 36
whale-shark 11
whales 7: baleen 11, 58, 59–60, 69,
  87; beluga 198; blue 36, 59–60,
  78; calving 171; coastal 174;
  evolution 219; great 199; grey 78,
  191; human threat 78; humpback
  69, *87*; killer 11, *85*; minke 7, *87*;
  sperm 37
whelk, dog 174
Wilson's storm-petrel 80
wrasse *15*, 95, *97*; *see also* angelfish,
  groupers, parrotfish, tuskfish

Yap islands 197, *197*, 199, 200, *212*

zooplankton 11, 36, 58, 59, *65*, 65,
  66
zooxanthellae (algae) *25*, 173